Out of My Comfort Zone

Retired Teacher Experiences Living, Teaching, and Traveling Abroad

A memoir by

Carol Coffey

Published in the United States of America.
First Edition.

Book Cover Designed by Carol Coffey.

Library of Congress Cataloging-in-Publication Data:
Coffey, Carol
Out of My Comfort Zone: Retired Teacher Experiences Living, Working, and Traveling Abroad / Coffey, Carol – 1st edition - 145 pages

Self-published by Carol Coffey
ISBN number: 1453899936
EAN-13 is 9781453899939.
(Trade Paperback)

1. Coffey, Carol—Travel, 2. Traveler's Writings, American 3. Germany: social life and customs—21st century 1. Title

This book is a memoir based on the author's recollections.

Carol Coffey
Colorado Springs, Colorado
carolcoffeyphotography.com

Dedicated to and in loving memory of
Alice Ellis,
my friend and my inspiration.

Acknowledgements

I would like to thank my parents for all the care packages they sent, their emotional support throughout the journey, and for printing and saving my emails! What would I have done without them?

And I want to thank my daughter, Erin, for reading and editing the whole book, and writing the book description. Her knowledgeable comments and common sense suggestions have been incredibly helpful and have made the book much better. I could not have finished this project without her motivational support; continuing to tell me it was interesting, and that she was anxious to hear more.

I also want to thank my daughter, Krysta, for encouraging me to do this project and for visiting me while I was in Germany, making my experience more memorable. My appreciation goes out to all the amazing people I met on this journey, the friends who made it all so wonderful, and my students who were so incredible.

Preface

There is the risk you can't afford to take
And there is the risk you can't afford not to take. By Peter Drucker

This message, on a bookmark I have hanging on the wall, was my inspiration as I took the risk to leave my secure job in Colorado so I could take the risk I couldn't afford not to take; the opportunity to teach in a bilingual bicultural German public school in Berlin for two years.

At the age of 56, I was single again and my daughters were living their adult lives in other states. I took an early retirement from a teaching job, sold the house I couldn't afford, sold my furniture and numerous acquired possessions, stored some keepsakes, and flew to Europe for a new adventure.

Out of My Comfort Zone is dedicated to my good friend, Alice Ellis (LittleAli), who faithfully printed all my emails while I was working abroad. Always environmentally aware, she recycled on the back side of used papers and on my return presented these to me in a notebook with the challenge, "Write a book!"

Sadly, Alice learned she had ovarian cancer just after I returned to Colorado. She fought diligently but lost the battle almost two years later. She is my inspiration for this memoir. Memories of her sweet spirit are still alive in my world.

I have chosen to write this story in the form of emails to Alice, partly because this casual personal style of writing is my favorite, and mostly because it was a way to include Alice in this memoir.

Remembering everything as it had happened has been a challenge, but I had Alice's emails from the time she got her computer half way through the first year. She also included my letters in the notebook, which were a good resource. For some reason I deleted all my own emails and only kept a journal on a few holidays, but my thoughtful parents printed and saved every email I sent them. My father always deletes emails from his computer, but prints the important ones so mother can read them at her leisure. In 2003 I was astonished when I asked if they had any of my old emails. Mother said, "Sure, they're right here."

Alice had passed away and I knew I needed to somehow honor her challenge and write that book! My other sources of information were printed information, trip brochures, pictures, and a few letters to friends that were still on my computer. To the best of my knowledge, memory, and understanding, the whole story is true, including the names and places, which I think are spelled right. Some of the dates may be a little off but I think they are very close to the actual ones.

HOW MY GERMAN ADVENTURES BEGAN

New Year's Eve is a time of reflection and goal setting for me. I've found I prefer a quiet time alone with my thoughts, prayers and dreams for the coming year on that night when the rest of the world is celebrating and partying.

On New Year's Eve, 1998, I was living in the mountains near Divide, Colorado. My house was on a hill at 9000-ft elevation. The Collegiate Peaks 90 miles away were visible to the West from my bedroom window. A full view of the "back side" of 14,000-ft. Pikes Peak was my view from the guest room window. At midnight on New Year's Eve, fireworks are set off from the top of Pikes Peak. A group of rugged individuals called *The AdAmAn (Add a Man) Club* annually backpack to the top and set off fireworks for the city of Colorado Springs to the East and all the people within view of that famous peak. I had a warm and cozy ringside seat for watching that colorful display.

From the beginning of this school year, I had decided it was time to retire from teaching in Colorado and do something else. I didn't have a clue what I wanted to do. I just needed a change and knew I wanted to travel and that I wanted to work with kids again. I had been teaching math and then computers in high school, junior college, and middle school for 25 years and had worked with kids for 23 of those years. My current position had evolved to one of *technology curriculum specialist* and I did not have classes to teach anymore. Although I loved my job, I did miss working with the students on a regular basis, so when I was making my goals for 1999, one of them was to retire from teaching in Colorado and to have a job where I travel outside the United States and work with kids.

If I were going to retire, I'd need to move. So I needed to sell my house. I loved that house. I especially loved the views of rainbows, lightening in the mountains to the west, fog creeping in to surround me like a hug from God, morning mist rising from the valleys, abundant colorful wildflowers, 30 inch snows blanketing everything in sight, brilliant sunsets, and the elk, deer, fox, hummingbirds, and porcupine that made regular visits to my "Wind Dancer Ridge." I had called a realtor during Christmas break and told him to list my house for sale. If it sold before summer, I would need to rent, but I thought I 'should" list it early "just in case".

I also knew I needed more money. I wasn't able to make ends meet on my current salary of $35,000, and my retirement salary would be little more than half of that, so I knew I had to have more money. Feeling especially brave on New Years Eve, I decided to ask for $75,000 annual salary. I have no idea why that number popped into my head, and when it did, I thought it was pretty ridiculous to be asking for such a high amount, but I wrote it down anyway. I had been listening to Jack Canfield's tape, *Self-Esteem and Peak Performance*, and felt inspired.

I love mountains and have always wanted to visit Nepal, that magical kingdom home of Mt. Everest and a multitude of other high Himalayan peaks. Not being in 'peak' mountaineering condition, I had found a trip to Nepal I could physically do. It involved a little trekking as well as touring a variety of tourist sites and ancient cities there. I really wanted to go but knew the $4000 price tag was $4000 more than I had. As a teacher, I had never had extra money to save. But I decided while I was setting goals, I might as well include that one in my list as well. As I did it, I was thinking, "You want to quit your job, have half your present insufficient income, and go where? for how much money? I don't think so!" But I'd just purchased Wayne Dyer's tape program, *Manifest Your Destiny*, and I knew anything was possible. He says, "If you believe it, you see it." and I really wanted to believe it. So my fourth resolution was to travel to Nepal. I had never traveled outside the United States until 1998. It was a fantastic Swiss hiking trip with the Colorado Mountain Club and I thought I would never be financially able to travel again.

So my 1999 Goals became:

1. Retire from teaching in Colorado and get a job where I can travel and work with kids.
2. Sell my house.
3. Receive $75,000 annual salary.
4. Travel to Nepal.

When I make goals I meditate and pray about it. Jesus said "Ask and you shall receive." Scripture which follows indicates that we must also believe. In another message, he tells us to have the faith of the mustard seed. When I set my goals, I pray "I ask that ……" Then I try to believe my dreams will be fulfilled. Sometimes that is hard, but it gets easier as I witness miracles and answered prayers in my life.

What a magical year '99 became! First, the house didn't sell for a long time. I was actually happy because I loved it so much and had faith it would sell at the right time. I had only put it on the market so early out of fear that I *should.* I told my principal and friends I would be retiring at the end of the school year, so the die was cast.

When I went to have my taxes done in early February, my tax accountant told me I shouldn't sell the house until I'd lived there two years, which would be April 19th. If I sold before that, I'd need to pay taxes on all profit including profit from the condo I had sold two years before. I was so relieved I hadn't had an offer yet, and I immediately called the realtor and told him to put it on hold until late April.

Getting my taxes done was really fun that day! I had saved back $4000 to pay the taxes from the sale of a cabin I had received as part of my earlier divorce settlement, so I didn't worry too much about what I would owe. However, I had had some large medical expenses that year, and was consequently able to take a large deduction for them. When he told me I didn't owe any money, I couldn't believe it! I excitedly said "I'm going to Nepal!" That trip cost $4000—the same amount I was planning to hand over to the government for taxes! Was I ever a happy taxpayer!!!!!! When I got home I got on the Internet and signed up for that trip! I just could not believe my luck! I did go traveling, sightseeing, and trekking in Nepal in May and was so touched by the sweet-spirited, gracious, hard working Nepalese people and the majestic beauty of their land.

Near the end of February I received an email which had been received by a media specialist in Fort Collins, Colorado. She forwarded it to our district media specialist, who then forwarded it to all the technology curriculum specialists in our school district. It simply stated there was an opening for an American computer teacher in Berlin, Germany for a 2-year position. When I got the email, I thought, "This is it! I want to do that!" Suddenly I had energy! Passion! Nothing could stop me! I immediately called the personnel director; got the information I needed, sent in my application, called my principal and district technology director for recommendations, and was called for in interview in Fort Collins in two weeks. The principal of the school and the Berlin Superintendent of Schools were touring the United States for International Schools' job fairs and stopped in Fort Collins to interview me.

Although I was told I'd hear in three weeks, I received the call in one week. I had told everyone I wasn't sure I'd accept, I still had lots of questions that needed to be answered and if offered the position, I'd just ask for a week to think it over. However, when I picked up the phone and the principal said, "You wanta come to Germany?" My immediate response was an enthusiastic "**Yes!**" No doubts, no questions, just a definite 'yes'. I would be there in August. I never regretted the decision; I had a wonderful two years teaching at John F Kennedy Schule, a bicultural, bilingual Berlin Public School. I was teaching computers to elementary children in grades 3, 4, 5 and 6. I loved that position, it seemed perfect for me

Germans love to travel and believe in long vacations from school. The money was good and I had the vacation time, so I was able to travel throughout Germany, to Poland, to the beautiful city of Prague in the Czech Republic, and Norway, Sweden, Denmark, Switzerland, France, Italy, Spain, Mallorca, Tunisia, Turkey, Greece, and Egypt. So goal number one was met in the best of ways.

Oh, and the money! You won't believe this, but my German salary was approximately $56,000 dollars (depending on the exchange rate each month). Add that to my $19,000 retirement check and that's pretty close my $75,000 goal. And as an added bonus, the German salary was not taxable in either country the first two years.

I had put the house back on the market in late April. I made arrangements with a friend to stay with her after my house sold until I left for Germany the end of July. But the house just didn't sell. I got frustrated with the realtor and decided to sell it myself. I advertised and answered phone calls, gave directions, and almost had a buyer. That's when the county road-graders decided to grade my dirt roadbed. That meant the hard pack that had built up over the winter had to be packed down again. But the rains came, and that muddy road was impassable without 4-wheel drive. The prospective buyers couldn't get to my house, so they backed out. In June I listed with another realty company, we had an open house but it rained again and very few people could make it up my hill.

By then I was hoping I could stay in the house long enough to see the wildflowers bloom the beginning of July. I had scattered wildflower seeds in the snow in April two years earlier. About 30 beautiful varieties came up. They multiplied the next year. I was hoping they'd be even more bountiful this year, so when the wildflowers started blooming; I was saying a prayer of thanks every day as new ones came up. By then I just thought I was being Divinely cared for and that the house would sell at the right time. I had a huge sale of my furniture and all the extras I had accumulated.

Three weeks before leaving the country, I flew East to visit my family in West Virginia. The night before I left home, I heard a loud noise on my porch at 11 pm after I'd gone to bed. I turned on the porch light and saw a man standing there, looking away from the house to the mesmerizing view of the full moon over Pikes Peak. I called through the door to ask what he was doing there. He said he was interested in buying the house and the realtor had told him I wasn't home. He just wanted to see what it was like out there at night. He could not have chosen a better night, I totally understood his desire to check it out; it's what I would have done in the same circumstances. Right then, I knew that house, with the surrounding views and full moon, had sold itself. When the phone rang my second day in West Virginia, my realtor said I had an offer, I accepted, and *I closed on the house the day before I flew to Berlin.* What perfect timing; I got to stay in my house until the last night! I got to see all those new flowers bloom, and miraculously, a rainbow appeared in my field a few days before I left. It stayed there for 20 minutes, and I knew it was just for me, a promise that a Higher Power was with me and would be with me on my next adventure. And He was.

From: Carol
To: LittleAli
Subject: **Hooked Up and Plugged In!**
Date: Wednesday, August 11, 1999

Hi Alice,

I can't believe it took so long to get my computer working and to get my email here. What a relief! And it was so good to get connected and be able to hear from you again.

A lot has happened since I left Colorado Springs July 31st. Leaving my house was the most difficult but I feel so fortunate to have been able to stay in it till the night before I flew out. The closing was the 27th, I packed my car that morning in Divide, stopped in Woodland Park for the house closing, and took my leased Rodeo to the dealer (I hated to give up that car, great memories, lots of incredible 4-wheeling trips); their shuttle took me to a motel in Colorado Springs that afternoon.

As you know from our backpacking trips, I always pack everything I think I might possibly need, but this time I had to repack and leave a lot of good things behind at the motel. At 4am, I finished packing and slept soundly until 9am. A taxi took me to the airport and the flights went as scheduled. Such a relief! I was finally able to rest, to collapse into my seat and take a nap; to be at peace!

When I turned 50 I said I wasn't going to worry about what people thought of me anymore; I was going to do what felt right. Now I am 56 and free to fly to more new adventures than I could ever imagine! I have jumped out of my comfort zone into a whole new world!

The people from the school (John F Kennedy *Schule*) here in Berlin are so gracious and helpful—and very organized. I've been totally taken care of. My first official duty was to attend a gathering at a local Biergarten and meet our leaders and co-workers; we were officially hired with a handshake and received the Stemple of Approval from the Landesschulamt (Office of Education).

They are giving us (There are 18 new Americans teaching here this year; I am the oldest teacher in the group.) three weeks of orientation, helping us fill out a multitude of German forms, giving us medical tests, and introducing us to life here in the city too. Paperwork, policies and procedures—all perfectly prepared for even the most naive, like me. Registering with the Police, getting Residency Permits, registering TV's and Radios for a small quarterly fee (or—a huge fee if fail to register), opening Bank Accounts, and filling out forms with the school district are not easy tasks when they are in a foreign language, but it's not all work! We've been touring the city, stopping at cafes, meeting at *biergartens*, and having get-togethers. What a fun group of people with such varied backgrounds and exciting stories to tell!

My first technical challenge was the telephone, who would have thought! I wanted to call my parents and daughters immediately. There was a very old telephone here in the apartment. Guess what? It is not touchtone! It has the touchtone buttons but when you push them you hear a long dialing sound. There is nothing on the phone to switch it over like we have in the US. To dial directly from here is financial suicide so I needed to use an access code, which meant I'd only be paying 15 cents a minute to call home. But! That only works with touchtone phones!!!!! I couldn't get it set up with my dialing buttons. No problem, I thought, I brought a telephone with an answering machine in my luggage. I plugged the phone cord in—it is the same here as there, amazing! I got a dial tone, and I could dial. Great! I called the access code and that worked, I got it all set up, and made my call. I decided to plug in the answering machine part of the phone and realized I don't have a transformer yet; it's in my shipment, scheduled to arrive anytime in the next six months. Well, at least the phone worked—until I heard the old phone ring and noticed my phone didn't ring. I picked up my phone and it worked, it just doesn't ring without electricity. No problem, I'll use the old phone for the ringer and my own phone to dial and talk. Problem solved! But no answering machine yet.

I was totally surprised—my shipment came last week! Mine was one of the first to get here, way ahead of the predicted six months. My shipment was small enough to be sent via air for the same cost, lucky me! However, it has taken me a week to get hooked up! I couldn't believe how difficult that was; you'd think it would be a piece of cake for a computer teacher, wouldn't you? Not really! My computer was in good condition and I had switched the button on the back for European current, so I could just plug it in with the special cable. The monitor was ok for either voltage.

But everything else had to be plugged into the transformer. Seemed simple enough. Luckily, I didn't plug anything into the power strip to start with. I just plugged the power strip into the transformer and plugged the transformer into the wall outlet. **Then I turned on the transformer!** Wrong! All the lights went out, the power strip fried and I had to search for the *hausmeister* who speaks mostly Turkish mixed with some German. Of course it was night; I called Kevin, a fellow American, the tech teacher at the high school, who went with me to the apartment of the *hausmeister*. It's not easy explaining all I just told you in a language we don't know, but we pointed to the overhead light and said "kaput" and he understood ("*Ya, ya.*") and followed us to my dark apartment. He brought a fuse that didn't work. With the aid of my flashlight I found many different sizes and shapes of fuses. Viola! One worked and there was light! After talking it over with Kevin, we both realized I have to have the transformer turned on before I plug it into the wall. Otherwise it doesn't transform anything; it just sends strong German current into our meek little American appliances. Kevin's transformer didn't even have an on/off switch. I taped mine "on" just incase I forget later.

The next technological challenge was finding enough places to plug in all my electrical stuff. My apartment only has two wall outlets in the living room. So I needed to use a power strip. Thank goodness I put two in my shipment just in case. I had purchased all the furniture from the previous renters, so extension cords were available and put to good use. Most important of all was the dual phone adapter which, when used with my dual phone adapter from home, was enough to let me have the ringing phone and the dialing phone and the computer modem plugged in all at once. Everyone else has to get down on the floor, crawl under the furniture, unplug the phone and plug in the computer modem to do email and internet—awkward! I feel very adapter blessed!

All the doors are double locked; if you lock them from the inside, no one can get in even if they have a key, and you can't get out without a key, so people leave their keys in the lock when they're inside. I guess it's safer but seems paranoid to me. I don't see how that could work for two people who live in one apartment. They probably do what I do. I don't lock from the inside. I only lock the outside one, it's like we have at home. It seems like a very safe place, and if I get injured and can't get to the door, the hausmeister or a friend with a key could rescue me.

Now it's your turn to fill me in since I left. I miss you and I'm sorry you're missing all these challenges.

Till later,
Carol

From: Carol
To: LittleAli
Subject: **Traumatic TB Test Torture!**
Date: Thursday, August 12, 1999

During this orientation process, we also had some medical tests taken. The TB test was **traumatic**! Our mixed group of mostly young fit men and women with me being the fattest and oldest, were "herded" onto the train, into an old section of the city, down back streets, into a huge oppressive old dark brick building. In the spartanly furnished gray basement, we were sent into individual changing rooms to wait our turn. In broken English, the nurse told us to strip to our waists and wait till she called us to have our chest x-ray. Our little quarters had two doors, the one we went in and the one that opened into the huge open room with the x-ray machine. We could hardly hear our names called and I started to open the door to hear better—until I realized the others might need to do that too and I would be on display for all to see when my turn came. Actually I don't think any of them "peeked" and I got my "picture" taken and passed with flying colors (mostly blushing pink). The rest of the excursion was fun. We even climbed to the top of a tower to get a better view of the city.

The weather is beautiful, very warm, and is perfect for sitting outside at open cafes in the evenings. Most all restaurants have outdoor areas and very few people sit inside this time of year. I haven't noticed any air conditioning anywhere and it is in the 90's (Fahrenheit). I am comfortable in my apartment, the brick makes it well insulated and I can bring in the cool night air. Luckily I'm on second floor so I can have the windows open and still have privacy. I also don't get flies and bees like I would on first floor (which they call Ground Level—my floor is called First Floor.)

Get this! They don't have any window screens here. In fact, it's very common to see flies and bees in the bakery flying around under the glass counter and resting on the pastries. It doesn't seem to be an issue, they don't even shoo them off. The pastries and breads are delicious—and yes, I do shoo the flies off before I eat them.

From: Carol
To: LittleAli
Subject: **Airing My Laundry**
Date: Friday, August 13, 1999

I'm finding even the simplest things to be difficult here! Although I'm getting used to no car, microwave, or air conditioner, and toilets with no water until you flush; some things are more challenging.

I need to do a laundry but I'm afraid—the washer (which is in my kitchen) is little and has the door on the side. It empties into the kitchen sink when you're lucky. I'm afraid it may overflow and go into the apartment below and I don't have insurance till Sept 1st. Here, people are required to get liability insurance like we're required to get car insurance. I think it's mainly because the washers overflow so much and damage the apartments below. I've been doing clothes by hand but it's hard to do sheets and towels that way. There are no driers, so I have to hang clothes around the apartment and on a little folding dryer.

Get this, it's a law you can't use washing machines on Sundays, they are very loud, sound like an airplane taking off, and run for an hour. Germans say American washing machines just give our clothes a bubble bath. Running vacuum cleaners and hanging laundry on balconies are outlawed on Sundays too. Oh, and you can't take a shower from 10 pm to 6am, those are quiet hours every day. Gosh, I hope I don't get in trouble with the German police; it's hard to keep all the rules straight.

I'm really enjoying the people I work with. I didn't tell you yet about the afternoon I got here. I was picked up at the airport by a parent from the school. She is American but married a German and is living here and raising a family. She was very gracious, drove around the neighborhood, then offered to keep me overnight and for the first few days till my apartment was ready. I really wanted to be in my own space. Actually it worked out ok, the apartment had just been painted, all the furniture I had purchased from the previous renters (for $1000 in July) was stacked in the center and the carpet needed major cleaning. I was able to open the huge windows (I'm so excited, there are lots of windows so I can get all the ventilation I want!) and air out the rooms. There is a living room, one regular bedroom and one tiny bedroom, a bathroom, a kitchen, and two long halls—and lots and lots of doors. It seems Germans like to close off rooms, maybe to save heat. In my opinion, the interior doors are in the way and I'll have them open all the time. Unlike American apartments which are on one side of the building, these are all arranged so you have windows on opposite sides of the building, giving excellent cross ventilation.

Shortly after I got in the apartment, three of the new teachers, Ellen, Amy and Kirby showed up. They had been here longer and told me all about the area and all kinds of helpful tips. We had a great time sharing our stories and our excitement to have been among the "chosen" few. The next day, Amy, a young English teacher, took me to the S-Bahn (above ground commuter train) and showed me how to get a ticket. All those German words are Greek to me! I'll be using monthly tickets at first, but will get a yearly one August 31st. It is so inexpensive and they work for the bus and trains too. I'm so glad I decided not to get a car. What a free feeling this is!

Amy also took me to the local lake, Schlachtensee. We saw sunbathers—some with clothes, some without; families, children, and adults of all ages, sizes, and shapes. It seems like a normal neighborhood park but will take me awhile to get used to the nudity. And trust me; I will not be one of them! (Maybe when I as in better shape, but I'm beyond that now.) I know, "When in Rome…." but this isn't Rome and I can accept cultural differences without joining in.

I busted my butt getting my apartment arranged by bedtime that first night. You know I don't like clutter. This furniture is cheap! The couch is more like a wide canvas chair that can be adjusted to be like a flat hammock. It's very light weight and when I moved it into place and checked out the bed position, I laid down—and fell asleep instantly! Wow, that was a great nap! Guess I was tired—and I woke up with lots of energy!

It looks like some of the furniture is just stuck together—like the desk which has sides with drawers and a top which is not attached. I didn't know that. I moved the desk and the top fell on the big toe on my right foot! Ouch! I know it caused some damage—bruising at least—I got some ice from the frig and went back to work. Later, I decided to move that desk again—and guess what! The stupid top fell on the very same toe again! Hmm, guess it's not the top that's stupid! Here it is two weeks later, and that poor toe still hurts but I can walk without a problem.

When I was arranging my bedroom furniture, I started to put my underwear into the chest of drawers, but when I opened a drawer, I noticed it didn't have a back and rotated outward toward me! When I put anything in there, it just fell out the back. You can imagine how I was wondering what possible use this strange piece of furniture could have, and where was the real chest of drawers? Seeing nothing else that could work, I used duct tape and cardboard to make a back for this rotating now V-shaped drawer, and that's where my underwear and socks are living.*

---

*Later I learned this was a chest for storing shoes, but my shoes are staying on the floor.

From: Carol
To: LittleAli
Subject: **Berlin Boat Tour**
Date: Saturday, August 14, 1999

A group of us went sightseeing in the city today. We didn't know where we were going when we started; we just took the bus to the S-Bahn and got off downtown. We saw a sign about taking an English speaking boat tour down the river. We found the loading point and waited. We asked a lot of people but no one seemed to know. Boat tours stopped to pick us up, we said we wanted an English speaking tour, they said to take the next one. After about three hours, and turning down several tours, we decided the English ones didn't exist and took the next German tour. It was lovely, but we didn't know much about what we were seeing. So much construction is going on here, partly because Berlin is the new capital just as of this year, and partly because it has a lot of catching up to do since the wall went down in 1989. Most of the wall is torn down, they want the East and West to blend into one, but we did see where they left one part up as a memory. It's incredible to ride along and see the old bombed buildings, almost next to beautiful well-kept areas with lots of trees and gardens. This really is a beautiful city, with an unsettling history.

My feet hurt; I'm so drained and exhausted! I'm looking forward to a relaxing Sunday.

From: Carol
To: LittleAli
Subject: **Sunday Silence**
Date: Sunday, August 15, 1999

Well, it's Sunday! And guess what! Nothing is Open! The markets are closed, grocery stores are closed, all shops and stores are closed. Not only that, the stores in Zehlendorf, my nearest shopping area, closed at 1 pm on Saturday. The grocery store near her, Reichelt, closed at 2 pm yesterday. We could probably learn from de-emphasizing commercialism, I'm sure it promotes a healthier, more family-oriented lifestyle, but it's going to be hard for me to adjust!

There is one saving grace—the Shell Station on the corner is open! They're stocked with snacks, magazines, newspapers, fresh flowers, frozen dinners, liquor, wine, and some very unique last minute gifts, so what more could I need?

Restaurants are open and some of us are going to the beautiful Italian restaurant on the corner across from the Shell Station tonight. I'm really enjoying the food in the restaurants here, it's so fresh! Fresh Basil leaves are served on many dishes, all the cooked vegetables taste like they are cooked from fresh produce instead of frozen, and the salads are delicious. Of course I don't always know what I'm ordering because I can't read the language, but it always tastes fresh!

You probably know people shop daily for their fresh produce and breads at the little street markets and bakeries. That's also going to take some getting used to.

I called to talk to my girls today. With eight and seven hour time zone differences, that was a challenge. But it was great to hear their voices.

From: Carol
To: LittleAli
Subject: **I Got Paid!**
Date: Monday, August 16, 1999

I got paid! Yesterday in my mailbox at school, I got a slip saying the amazing sum of "0.00 dm" (that's deutschmarks) had been put in my checking account. I asked the school secretary about it, she really didn't know, so she said to check at my bank, maybe they had the money by then—and I did, and they did. I now know how to get my statement at the bank (via a machine—you can get it daily if you want).

When I told Krysta about my big paycheck, she commented, “Wow! Can you believe that you get the exact same amount as you did for raising Erin and me?”

I also paid my electric bill. You take the bill and the completed transfer form to the bank—they transfer the money to the electric company. You don’t even need to do it in person; you can put the form in the slot outside the building. But getting the numerals right is a challenge for me. The 7 must have a horizontal line through the middle; otherwise it looks like the 1. The reason it would look like the 1 is because the 1 must have a slanted flag at the top left, like the 7 does. The 4 is pointed like this typed one and the 9 is all curved like this typed one. I have to pay the electric bills every two months, and it's what they estimate I'll be using (based on the family of three who were in my apartment last year). After several months, if I haven't used that much electricity, I'll get some money credited back to me.

So much of what I have to spend is out of my hands—all handled by the bureaucracy. Actually none of us knew how much we'd be getting paid until we got our statements. There was no published salary schedule and no contract until we got here to shake hands. The shaking hands was the important part and August 1st was our first official day of work. Since August 1st was on a Sunday, we had to be at a specific restaurant at a specific time on that day (it was a beer garden and we had a great time!).

Thankfully, the amount of my salary was very close to the estimate I was given in the interview; same for all of us. Nearly all the banking is done by electronic transfer. They don't give you checks unless you request them, and then only 10 at a time. That's a good thing because I wouldn't have a clue how to spell the words of the dollar amount.

I was given a Eurocheck card (EC card)—good for Eurodollars* or Deutsche Marks. It is a debit card. I can use it at any of my bank locations or two other banks around here, at their machines in their entryways, for free—or at any other bank or ATM machine for a fee. They don't give you anything to keep a record on, and don't even understand when I ask. So I'll have to make up a way to keep my own records, as I'd like to know my balance, is that too much to ask? If I withdraw or electronically overspend, they give me 400 dm to cover it. One of the teachers needed money Friday, his money hadn't been deposited yet, so the bank gave him several hundred dm to tide him over for the weekend.

We have been filling out forms to have most of our expenses automatically taken from our accounts. It should be easier if it works. I'm not a believer yet.

Gotta go check my bank account!
Carol

---

*The Euro didn't really come into general use until after I left Germany in 2001 so I think I only used Deutsche Marks.

From: Carol
To: LittleAli
Subject: **OV (Original Version Movie)!**
Date: Wednesday, August 18, 1999

Tonight I'm going to see *Notting Hill* with Gretel, the elementary school librarian. She's German but speaks English fluently. We found a place that has a movie in its original version, English! Most American movies are dubbed in German; I'd have tremendous trouble following that! It seems strange that seeing a movie in my own language would be so exciting, but it is here!

My parents are sending me a care package. There are several things I'm having trouble finding here, so I've put in my request. They're sending little packets of instant Oatmeal. We were told things sent here should not be re-saleable so I'm asking mother to take them out of the box and put them in a zip lock bag. I've also asked for a couple of large boxes of Baking Soda, I can only find tiny One Tablespoon packets here. I use baking soda to clean with and to deodorize so I need more. I don't think it would be wise for the soda to be taken out of the package though, they might think it's cocaine or something toxic or dangerous.

Getting a package here is a pretty big deal, I think. We were told nothing should be declared worth more than $50 or we'd have to go to customs, somewhere far away, and pay big fees. We were also told our packages should not be insured either, it wouldn't help but it could call attention to its value and might be sent to customs. I also can't deal with a large package because I have to carry it a long distance and then on the train and bus. Since I wouldn't be here when it was delivered, I'll have to go to a post office to get it, I don't know where the post office for this area is yet; more to learn.

Our weather is getting cooler now at night. How's the Colorado weather? I'm going to miss the Aspen trees this fall but I'm hoping Berlin will have some colorful leaves too.

From: Carol
To: LittleAli
Subject: **ESL class**
Date: Thursday, August 19, 1999

Surprise! I thought I was hired to be the Computer Teacher at the Elementary School. Well, that's not all! Today, six days before school starts, I learned I am teaching a class of English to German students everyday! Help! I didn't know until I saw my schedule and went to ask about it. I thought I was overwhelmed already, with setting up the lab and all the computer classes and training. I really do want to do a good job, wish me luck.

But now that I think about it, I am technically qualified to teach an English Class. I am certified to teach Computers, Math, and English and have taught English in High School a very long time ago.

Freaking out here,
Carol

From: Carol
To: LittleAli
Subject: **Talking Trash**
Date: Friday, August 20, 1999

Orientation has been so busy; I didn't get to work in my classroom (computer lab) till today. That was overwhelming! All the computers were covered with lots of plastic and also with yards and yards of fabric. Guess what I found under there? Apple Macintosh computers! I was expecting Windows 98 PC's. That was a shock! I've been trained on the PC's; I've never seen a Mac! Now I know why the principal didn't answer when I asked at the interview what kind of computers he had. They look new and there are enough for each student. I hear they're really easy to use, so I'll learn!

In the back of the room and around the edges, the lab is filled with old Apple IIe computers and millions of those big floppy disks that are totally obsolete now. I hope they'll let me get rid of them. The walls have dusty faded posters about how to use those ancient machines; I think I need to find posters to liven up the place, mountain pictures of course. I'm going to email Bonnie and ask her to get me some at the Garden of the Gods Nature Center. She went there with me and knows the ones I want. I'm missing the Colorado Mountains already! I think the kids will enjoy seeing Mt Sneffles and Mt. Potosi with the Columbine wildflowers.

From: Carol
To: LittleAli
Subject: **Martin's Hometown**
Date: Sunday, August 22, 1999

Yesterday I went with Gretel to Wittenburg—have you heard of it? It's Martin Luther's old hangout. We visited the church where he posted his declaration on the door and began the reformation, consequently starting the Protestant Church. She drove her car; it's the first time I've been in a car since I got here. Driving the autobahn was a special treat, didn't seem like anyone was speeding, they all seemed to be in their lanes and following all the rules very well. Actually, Germans are excellent at that.

Wittenburg (Pronounced Vittenburg because there is no "w" sound in the German language and all W's are pronounced like V's; the V's are pronounced like F's; Volkswagen is pronounced folksvagen.) is a beautiful Medieval looking village. I really enjoyed walking down the streets and exploring these incredibly historic buildings. It's amazing to realize the world changes that have started in this small isolated town in Germany. Of course the Reformation had a huge impact on religion but also, in 1983, a small group of students met here and started making swords into plowshares, which was the beginning of the end of the cold war and the collapse of the Berlin wall.

Outside of town, their local high school, called *Hundertwasser schule*, sports the most artistic and innovative architecture I've ever seen. The design is very colorful and childlike with the columns looking like painted tinker toys, whimsical shapes and bright colors adorning the windows and doors and at entrances. Big colorful scarves hanging from the roof and turrets and towers make it look like a fairyland or a Dr Seuss illustration.

After getting out into the countryside yesterday, I've had to hunker down today and prepare for teaching. Gotta do it!

From: Carol
To: LittleAli
Subject: **First Day of Classes**
Date: Wednesday, August 25, 1999

I had a great first day of teaching today although I had only one class, the English one to the 4th grade German students! All of them understand and can speak some English already. Thank goodness, I'm only to speak English to them. The kids are just so sweet and cute and enthusiastic and polite, I think I'm really going to love this year. After teaching middle school and high school and community college, I'm finding these elementary aged children to be refreshing and a real delight. Hope that feeling lasts!

The computer lab is still a mess and needs much work. The dust is very deep, the printer didn't work today and I don't know the network or the passwords yet. Thank goodness my computer classes don't start till Monday.

This school is a Berlin Public School built right after the war to help Germans and Americans understand each other from a young age. Bilingual and bicultural, half the teachers and administrators are German and half are English speaking, mostly American. Half the students are German and half are English speaking, but all German students are basically bilingual by 4th grade. The school follows the standards of German schools and of the Fort Collins School District in Colorado. This is like a beautiful college campus, with several separate buildings: elementary, high school which includes 7th and 8th grades as well as grade 13, the counseling building, and the gymnasium.

In the meantime, my social life has been pretty good. I just got back from having dinner at another Italian restaurant with Lisa, a teacher from Hawaii who taught in Guam. Last night Susan and Kevin, a couple from Maine and Connecticut who taught in Norway took me to a wonderful Chinese restaurant only three blocks away. The food was so fresh and tasty, but best of all, they serve free plum wine before the meal. I think I'll be walking to that restaurant often.

Yesterday I had lunch off campus with Gretel, the German librarian, and her assistant, Pat. The schedules and expectations are really different here; we are only expected to be at work when we have a class scheduled. Each day has a different schedule and some days are longer than others. If we have time, we can have a long lunch in Zehlendorf or leave for any reason. Monday I had lunch with Laura, an English teacher from the U. S. who has been here a year already. I'm meeting many people who will probably become good friends.

The weather is beautiful now, high of 75, I think. I'd better get to work on my schoolwork now.

From: Carol
To: LittleAli
Subject: **High School Angel!**
Date: Friday, August 27, 1999

My worries about the computer lab network are taken care of. No one seemed to know anything, passwords, how the network worked, or anything—until today! An ANGEL named Jason appeared and took over!!! A high school student, he told me all about the system, which he had set up for the last teacher, and helped me with everything I needed to know. What a blessing he is! He says he'll be back in to help if I want—I do. You can't believe how happy I was to see him. I'd better equip the lab with snacks for the next time he's here.

There's a party tonight—a pot luck TGIF at Peggy's. She's the video queen, I understand. She's been here a year and is an American who has taught in Saudi, Kenya, and England*. She's been here a year already and is agreeable to loaning out her videos to the 'movies in English' starved newcomers.

---

*Peggy went to Turkey when she left Berlin.

From: Carol
To: LittleAli
Subject: **Shopping Day**
Date: Saturday, August 28, 1999

Finally, a Saturday! I had time to go shopping for teaching supplies. I got everything at the local Woolworth store, which closed at 1 pm of course. After sleeping in till 10 and taking the bus to get to Zehlendorf (the closest shopping area), I didn't have much time. I also had to rush back to go to the grocery store, Reichelt, which is just a block away from the apartment, by 2 pm when they closed.

The grocery shopping experience is a little different here. We always have to have one deutschmark (dm) coin (worth about 50 cents) to put into the lock that holds the grocery carts. You can't get a cart without a coin. When you return the cart, you get your coin back and you keep it with you at all times, just like a credit card and in the US and your drivers' license. I'm learning what's important! And when you shop for produce you must weigh it yourself. When it's on the scale, you need to find the name of the item (difficult for the language-challenged) and punch in its code. A sticker will come out of the scale; you place that on your produce so the checker will know the price when you check out. The first time, I didn't know to weigh and get the code. The cashier was not patient, and wouldn't let me through the line until someone came to help, take me back, and teach me the right way to process the produce!

Sometimes I can't find what I'm looking for because I don't know the name and can't ask. Today I was looking for matches. They weren't in any of the places I would expect, I tried to explain what I wanted with sign language, that didn't work. Matches and baking soda have both been a real challenge for me. Today I wanted some cinnamon. I looked through all the spices, surely I could tell by the color, the texture, or a similar word. Nope, I had to give up. I looked it up when I got home—it's spelled *Zimt*. The spices had been alphabetized and I had given up before I got to the Z's. But now I know. And champagne is called Sect, but wine is wein but pronounced, vine, of course. And get this: American Pizza from the frozen food section is topped with CORN!

I have a little folding fabric cart on wheels for my groceries. It came with the apartment; a definite necessity here. When folded, it looks like a baby's umbrella stroller. The two deep pockets hold enough groceries for a couple of days; nothing like in the United States where we fill our car and carry in sacks of groceries once a week. I also wear a backpack to work and can pick up produce or deli meats and salads as I walk to catch the bus and then the train after work.

We're going out on the town tonight—it's museum night and we get into all the museums for one low price.

From: Carol
To: LittleAli
Subject: **Museum Night**
Date: Sunday, August 29, 1999

That museum night on the town was amazing! A group of us rode the bus/train/bus to downtown Berlin and visited four different museums. I can sure tell I'm the oldest in the group, these young people can run to catch the busses. I go as fast as I can, but my body just gives out if I try to run, my legs feel like they're melting into the sidewalk and my chest feels like it's going to explode. I guess you could say they run ahead to hold the bus for me, but there is no guarantee the driver will wait. Still confused about which buses to take, I'm learning and it's exciting to keep going to new locations.

My favorite was the Pergamon, a Greek museum dating back to 1400 BC. It has artifacts the Greeks have been trying to get back. Whole walls and gates about three stories high from ancient Greek cities, along with 30 ft tall statues, made it feel like I was in ancient Greece. I couldn't read the German signs, but some of the cities sounded Biblically familiar.

We also visited the Berlin Dome (*Berliner Dom*), which looks like a cathedral. It's so incredibly beautiful inside; so awe-inspiring. They have concerts there and I learned our school will be performing in it at Christmas. I am impressed and excited!

Today I'm preparing for my first computer classes—I guess it's about time I did that.

From: Carol
To: LittleAli
Subject: **First Package!**
Date: Tuesday, August 31, 1999

My computer classes got off to a great start. I am teaching 4th, 5th and 6th graders. The 4th graders focus on keyboarding and are learning basic skills along with that. The older classes have flexible scheduling and come with their teachers to do projects related to that teacher's curriculum. I teach them the computer and software skills needed for each project. My goal is to integrate computers into the curriculum for every 5th and 6th grade classroom.

My parents sent me a care package, it wasn't hard to get at all. Such a relief! The package was actually left at the door of my apartment; I don't know how I got so lucky. Two friends who live here said their packages are always left at one of two post offices, which are not nearby, and sometimes at a distant customs office.

Everything was in perfect condition, the baking soda boxes didn't even bust. They sent candles and my favorite candies and some 5x7 picture frames. Picture frames here are different shapes and sizes from our standards, and don't fit my pictures. The package was extremely expensive to mail, but when you consider how much it would cost to personally deliver, I guess it's a good deal.

From: Carol
To: LittleAli
Subject: **Check Point Charlie**
Date: Saturday, September 4, 1999

Today Lisa and I went to the Check Point Charlie Museum. It's so powerful! The walls were filled with pictures of people trying to get over the Berlin wall, babies being passed over to be with their family, family members trying not to be separated, people riding in fake car gas tanks, people transported in suitcases, and people crawling through hand-dug tunnels. A group of people made a hot air balloon just from scraps around the house and books they read—and actually made it over the wall! I was appalled at pictures of people getting shot, people who didn't make it and their stories, and relieved to see those who helped get people across. So much terror and panic on the faces! It was haunting and inspiring; and you know me, I couldn't keep the tears from flowing half the time.

We're so lucky to live in a free country, and the people here now are so very lucky compared to the way it was just 10 years ago. Nov 9th marks the 10th anniversary of the wall coming down; a big celebration is being planned. I vividly remember watching television and seeing the young people on the wall, tearing it down brick by brick; who would have thought I'd be here 10 years later. It was such an exciting time, so much to celebrate!

After leaving the museum, we came home past a huge lake near here called Wannsee where we changed from the S-Bahn to a local bus. It's so beautiful, with large tourist boats, sail boats, other boats, and beautiful homes along the shore. We ate at an elegant restaurant along the lake. My stuffed Parmesan Zucchini with boiled potatoes, tomatoes and cucumber were so fresh and delicious. I loved eating outside along the lake, enjoying the warm evening and the lakeside views.

From: Carol
To: LittleAli
Subject: **Polish Pottery**
Date: Sunday, September 5, 1999

I got outta town and rode in a van!!! A few of the teachers who came here last year purchased a van together. Today I was invited to join them on a drive into Poland! The green rolling hills of the countryside reminded me so much of West Virginia and Kentucky. The roads were two lane paved; except for the illegible signs, I felt right at home.

Getting across the border was slow. We had to wait in line about an hour; then show our passports. Luckily we had no trouble. While waiting, I had time for creative visions of border crossings gone bad.

Just beyond the border, we kept seeing scantily dressed, questionably fashionable, young women; women standing along the highway all alone. It took awhile, but the more knowledgeable in our group informed us we were seeing prostitutes just doing their job. There were a lot of trucks on that highway; I guess the ladies knew where best to market their skills.

Our destination was a Pottery Factory near a tiny town about 40 miles down the road. Oh, that was fun! The pottery was all white with blue designs. So Polish! I'm being very careful with my money and don't want to ship a lot of things home, so just bought a few bowls and spoon and tea bag holders*. My friends got whole sets of dishes and serving pieces too.

On the way back, the border crossing into Germany was much quicker. We stopped for dinner and I had my first German French fries. They are called *Pommes Frites* and are much better than ours, probably because they are fresher and use healthier oil. This is something I will need to ration, it could easily become addictive.

---

*I still have the Polish Pottery and use it every day. It comes with sweet memories and a special feeling of gratitude.

From: Carol
To: LittleAli
Subject: **Hitzefrei!**
Date: Friday, September 10, 1999

How cool is this? We got out of school at noon today because it was too hot! The temperature was 77 degrees Fahrenheit at 11am. When that occurs, we get Hitzefrei, a free afternoon out of school. With no air conditioning in the schools, I guess they think it would be too warm. It feels comfortable to me.

Actually I am really enjoying teaching here, the students are so precious and well mannered; both the German and English speaking ones. The computer lab is really working well; those new Macintosh computers are a pleasure to work with and the network connecting all of them allows me to give students individual folders for their work and gives me amazing control over all the machines. My presentations can show up on every computer if I want, or I can put a form, document, or image on each computer for them to work on.

The old equipment is still piled in the back, but my new mountain posters lift our spirits. Now I'm thinking I'll email Mary and ask for cute baby animal posters I had seen in Mueller State Park. I'm sure the students will enjoy them as much as I will.

From: Carol
To: LittleAli
Subject: **Going on a Cruise!**
Date: Tuesday, September 14, 1999

I had a good day at work, have another Parents' night tomorrow, and must prepare tonight for it. The parents are very supportive and interested, so it's fun but I need to be on my toes.

Tonight Laura and I went out to another Italian Restaurant close by, then over to Lisa's to see the brochure for the Mediterranean Cruise we've already signed up to take Fall Break. At first there were six of us going; now there are 10. Some of us fly; some take a train, to Milan, Italy. From there we take a shuttle to Genoa where we board the ship. The cruise goes to Naples; the island of Sicily; Tunis, Tunisia (Northern Africa); Barcelona, Spain; the island of Mallorca; Marseilles, France; then back to Genoa.

We'll tour the cities and sights by day and cruise and sleep by night. I saw a picture of the ship—just like the "Love Boat." I've never seen boats like that in real life. I'm so excited!

We leave October 16 if it's a Saturday.

Your Pancake Rocks hike sounds wonderful; it's one of my favorite spots on the back side of Pikes Peak—with one exception—when I broke my ankle near the top of Pikes Peak and had to walk down four miles on it. You and the other girls were so helpful: finding the walking stick, Jan's shoulder to hold onto, dipping bandannas in the stream to keep me from fainting. Although the lightening was frightening, the hail helped cool me off and made our trail an icy cold stream which slowed the swelling and numbed the pain! And I'll never forget the rainbow greeting us at the car! Even that trauma was somehow a spiritual experience and I appreciated all your help.

From: Carol
To: LittleAli
Subject: **Rainy Days**
Date: Monday, September 27, 1999

I had a good and relaxing weekend, going out to dinner twice and to a movie (OV….original version……English speaking……made in America) in downtown Berlin. Otherwise I stayed in and did school work.

Erin called around 2am last night. With this six hour time difference, my daughters don't have time to talk with me when I'm awake. But I'm not picky, just hearing from them is terrific! Erin is in Connecticut doing an Internship in her senior year of college. Right now, she has trouble even finding a phone to call on. Krysta, my engineer daughter, does have a phone and can even send email so we are in contact more often.

The long distance calling has been a challenge and a learning experience. It is very expensive to just call using my regular phone service, T-1. One of our group is fluent in German and has kept us informed of the cheapest rates for code calling. Using touch tone, we dial a very very very long number before dialing the country code, area code, and the phone number. The call only costs about 15 cents or less per minute and is automatically charged to our T-1 phone bill. I have even programmed the most recently least expensive code into my computer for dialing the AOL internet phone connection. I don't use the internet much and for email I download, disconnect, then read and answer at my leisure, and upload fast to send. It's been much better than using an internet provider here. I am paying AOL with my American Visa card automatically, and they probably don't even know or care that I'm out of the country.

I heard Colorado had snow yesterday, are you enjoying it? I hear we don't get much here and I do miss it. It's been raining. Tonight I had a meeting after school. I'm considered important (can you believe that?). It's only for administrators and department leaders. Since I am the Technology Coordinator for the Elementary School, my presence is required. Since it was raining, the principal drove me to the train and saved me about a 10 minute walk. I'm especially grateful because it's been windy and my umbrellas turn inside out! Other than being embarrassing, it's soaking too!

Did I tell you my daily commute includes a five minute walk to a bus stop, a 10 minute ride to the S-Bahn train for another 10 minute ride, then a 10 minute walk to school? I actually enjoy it and am so glad I don't need a car here.

I'm learning not to be so formal with the few German words I know. Instead of the formal *Auf Wiedersehen*, which I never hear, *Wiedersehen* (pronounced Ve' der zane) is used to say *Good Bye* or more often, Tschüs (pronounced *choose* with a little *t* sound in the beginning) meaning *Bye*. In the morning, I've learned to say *Morgen* instead of *Guten Morgen*, and most people say *Danke* instead of *Danke Schön* or Vielen *Dank* for *Thank You*.

I need to buy an extra set of sheets. Since we don't have driers and it's been so rainy and humid, my laundry, which is hung all over my apartment, is taking two days to dry, even with me rearranging them often.

Enjoy the snow! Your Vail trip to see the changing Aspen trees sounds divine! That is such a beautiful area and the *Wildflowers* are such a fun group. I do miss our hiking trips.

From: Carol
To: LittleAli
Subject: **Runaway Bride**
Date: Saturday, October 9, 1999

Mother sent sheets! This time I had to pick it up at the post office nearer my school, not the one nearer where I live. A note was on my door. It's such an adventure to get a package here!

Last night I went to see the movie, *Runaway Bride*, at Potsdamer Platz in downtown Berlin. Gretel drove her car, what a treat! We parked in the huge underground parking garage (parking spots are hard to find here, another reason I'm glad I don't have a car.) Luckily she could read the signs and could find our way to up to the theater. The movie was sweet. I heard someone in line behind us comment, "Of course it has a happy ending, it's an American Movie!" And they were right.

We had dinner in the mall; great oriental food! When I left her, I went down one level and walked underground to the S-Bahn and went home on it, and a bus of course. Going underground is much better; I usually go above ground and have to cross the huge street with so much construction. Since the wall came down, much of the old East Germany is being rebuilt and is becoming extremely modern. Huge cranes in big holes are everywhere; it's a project of monstrous proportions. The tunnels I walk in are very wide and well lighted and even have shops in them. Being a mountain girl, I've never seen so much concrete and I know my friends can't believe how unworldly I am. But I'm learning fast!!!

Lisa's grandmother sent her a video tape of the new TV show, *Providence*. It's great, I'd never seen it. When you're in a country where you can't understand the TV shows, getting one you do understand is such a treat!

Oh, that Moonlight Hike in Mueller State Park to hear the Elk bugling sounds great! I remember going there with you last year; it's a special place and a unique time of year to be there. Hmm—I also remember taking a few boyfriends to the park, but we never found the Elk. Oh well, we had good moonlight hikes.

From: Carol
To: LittleAli
Subject: **Mediterranean Cruise**
Date: Tuesday, October 26, 1999

I'm back! Fall Break is over, and I've cruised the Mediterranean!!! I feel so much more worldly now, like a world traveler.

The cruise was from October 14 – 21, a full week of traveling to new places. We first flew to Milan and spent the night. That was sweet. We were actually in the suburbs, a small town, and ate in an authentic Italian restaurant with the local people. We were the only tourists, and probably the only ones who could speak English. Restaurants didn't open till 7 pm; we were so hungry we walked a couple of miles trying to find one that was open. When we got back to that first one, it was 7 pm and the food could not have tasted better; definitely worth the wait. The taxi drivers are crazy and they ripped us off some. We called for two taxis, they came at the same time, three of us got in each taxi; we all went to the same airport from our hotel. One group got charged considerably more. When we disagreed with the price, they just kept saying "Is OK." They even got a policeman at the airport to come over and he said, "Is OK." Crooks! Oh well, it's only play money, right?

We took a bus to Genoa to leave for the cruise on Costa Romantica; not the biggest ship, but plenty big for me. It was wonderful, very luxurious, extremely clean, and run so efficiently. We traveled by night, were in ports during the day, and went sight-seeing in each country. I took tours everywhere because I wanted to see all I could. My roommate, Peggy, who had already been here a year, must have thought I was so naïve. She was very patient to explain so many things she took for granted. When I wanted to sign up for our daily tours before they were full, she was more relaxed and said she'd do it later. I think she was surprised (and probably relieved) when I did it by myself. We ended up taking some tours together and more separately. I'm becoming independent and it feels empowering! It especially amazes me because I was so naïve on my first trip outside the US and Canada—last summer—to Switzerland—for two weeks of hiking in the alps with the Colorado Mountain Club. I felt I was dragged through the airports by the rest of the group; now I can do it by myself!

After visiting Naples, I toured the ruins of Pompeii with Peggy and other friends. Walking through the ruins of this historic city was impressive but very sad. We also visited Palermo on the island of Sicily and I went through the gruesome catacombs and saw many awe-inspiring cathedrals too. It's a beautiful place of contrasts with proud people of many cultures and many languages.

Food on the ship was very plentiful and you could eat at anytime. Dinner, however, was only served at 7 and 9 pm. We had to sign up and have the same table and time every night. My friends wanted the late hour incase we got back late from our tours; I found it gave me indigestion and a restless sleep. Shows were after dinner, so we had some late nights. I did get in the routine and it all worked out. My friends didn't always go on tours, sunning at the pool and relaxing on the deck were their choices.

We had one very rough day on the sea while going across to Northern Africa (Tunisia). The distance was so far, we had to sail most of the day as well as the previous night. It was very difficult to walk and I had to hold onto railings to walk down the hall. I really felt sorry for servers at lunch;

they could just barely carry the food to the tables. Luckily I didn't get sick, many did. One of the gift shops had acupressure wrist bands that worked their magic! My friends who used them said it got rid of their seasickness in about 15 minutes—but one kept it on when she got off the ship and she started to get sick again until she took it off. Very interesting and definitely something I'll remember for friends in the future. I bought one to carry in my purse.

Finally arriving in Tunis in Tunisia, I toured ancient Carthage. It was very interesting and sometimes shocking. I bought my dad a souvenir picture book since it was Biblical, but after looking at it, I see some of the pictures are just not appropriate. Wall paintings and statues showed very well endowed men as well as scantily clad women he would not appreciate. I don't know what I'll do with that book.

We toured and shopped in the village of Sidi Bou Said, well known for their beautiful blue and white houses along the sea. We also shopped in the village—an experience much like Nepal—with people chasing you down the street bargaining with you to buy their wares. Those men can be quite obnoxious. One even followed me down the street and to the bus. He carried the wooden carved camel I had inquired about. The price was way too high. He kept coming down and I kept saying, "No." After I got in the bus, he came down to the price I had in mind, about one third of the first one, and I said, "Yes." and got out of the bus to pay him. Then he started a big sob story about how he needed the money and it was worth so much more, so I said, ok and started to leave without it. He immediately said my price again and I bought it. I'm learning but probably getting ripped off occasionally too.

I also bought a traditional Tunisian red dress with gold trim. It's full length, not fitted, short sleeved and beautiful. I will probably only wear it for Halloween, but I love it. The bus ride back to the ship was upsetting. I was on an English speaking tour, mostly British with the only Americans being a few of my friends. (There were five tours to each place, a different language for each.) Our tour guide was a sweet young British woman. The bus driver was Tunisian and played with our minds, making us think he wasn't going to get us back to the ship on time. I could tell our tour guide was very worried but tried to make him think she thought he was just teasing. We made it at the last minute. I did not appreciate his evil sense of humor. The ship has to leave, whether its passengers make it or not. It has a schedule to keep.

On the island of Mallorca, I visited Palma and took a bus trip up the coast to beautiful caverns. This is a very touristy place and doesn't have the European feel like other countries do. I think they lose their charm and authenticity when they cater so much to tourists. It is a very beautiful island and my claustrophobia must be gone; I was quite comfortable in the dark caverns and enjoyed being serenaded by boaters rowing up the underground river.

Barcelona, Spain was my favorite city; so artistic, with such grand Gothic cathedrals and incredible artistic masterpieces. The most incredible is *Sagrada Familia*, Antonio Gaudi's famous unfinished architectural achievement. Construction began in 1882 and it continues today. I can not begin to explain all the intricacies and shapes of this breathtaking creation. Our bus was detained about 15 minutes by protesters in the streets of Barcelona. The driver said it was a common occurrence and had allowed extra time for it.

A bus tour took me about an hour out of the city to Montserrat. That is truly my favorite part. It is a monastery in the rocky hills. I left the group and took a half hour hike into the rocks until it got too muddy and I ran out of time. Three hours was just not enough time for that scenic area. The Black Madonna statue is the biggest attraction; the Virgin Mary was supposed to have appeared there around 800AD. I saw a wedding, heard a boys choir sing in the cathedral, and just enjoyed being there, it had a good feel.

In Marseille, France, my tour went about an hour away to Avignon. The Popes Palace is there, and the famous Bridge of Avignon. I especially enjoyed just walking down the very narrow, curving, cobblestone streets with the brick houses right on the edge of the streets; not even room for a tiny blade of grass to make it up between the houses and the street. I don't see how a car can go on those streets; luckily none did while I was walking. I couldn't go around the block because the streets don't connect. It's like being in a maze; I had to go back the way I came. I really liked the little cafes too—and the wonderful ice cream (gelato).

On the last night, I began to panic and said I couldn’t go out that evening because I needed to pack my suitcase. It had been crammed full when I came, then I purchased a few treasures, so I feared it would not all go in. My roommate came to my rescue. She’s such a seasoned world traveler, so relaxed and knowledgeable. She said just to lay everything as flat as possible. I did, and it worked! That is a tip I could have used years ago, remember how much more luggage I took on our trips than you did. Of course I said it was because I was bigger, so my clothes took up more space.

I can't believe you hiked Cameron's Cone just west of Colorado Springs; I've heard it's really rough with lots of bushwhacking! I'm glad the snow wasn't very deep yet. Did you forget you're 69 years old? When are you going to grow up and act your age? Congratulations on making it up and down safely!

From: Carol
To: LittleAli
Subject: **In the News**
Date: Thursday, November 4, 1999

Hey, get this, I'm a celeb! I was interviewed by a *Rocky Mountain News* reporter today. He contacted our school for teachers from Colorado. There are two of us, so we were interviewed together. Being shy and very new here, I didn't have much to say, but all went well. The reporter is here for the Wall Celebration and wanted a Coloradoan's perspective. If you see it, I'd love to have a copy.

Tuesday, Nov 9, is the tenth year anniversary of the Berlin Wall coming down. That was such an exciting event; and now I'm here celebrating with the Germans! A big celebration will be held at the Brandenburg Gate (Tur) that evening. I think Bush and Gorbachev are speaking, and there's a concert.

Krysta has been working with the youth at her church in Baton Rouge and just attended a conference in San Diego to get more ideas and training. Erin is in Hartford working as an Intern in a theater until December, then back to college for her last semester. I'm so proud of them and although I wish I could be with them, I realize I wouldn't see them even if I were still in Colorado, except for a few days at Christmas.

That tour you took of Picketwire Canyon south of La Junta in Eastern Colorado sounds fascinating. I didn't even know about the dinosaur track way along the Purgatory River. I loved your description of footprints of moms and their young walking together in social groups. There's so much of Colorado I haven't seen yet.

From: Carol
To: LittleAli
Subject: **Bilingual TV**
Date: Saturday, November 6, 1999

Tired of not understanding the news here, I bought a new TV today so I could get an English speaking station. I went to an electronics store in Zehlendorf (nearest where I live) and bought their cheapest TV, had them call me a taxi, and rode home in luxury. The fee was only $7, so it was well worth it and much better than carrying a TV on a train, a bus, and walking a couple of blocks.

With the highest channel number of 13, the old TV couldn't bring in BBC on channel 18 or CNN on channel 26. This new one probably goes up to 100. I can now hear English, yea!

I am keeping the old TV to see my video tapes. It is attached to an American VCR, which plays my American video tapes. The video tapes and players are different here and won't work on an American system, and mine won't work on theirs.

From: Carol
To: LittleAli
Subject: **Preparing for Switzerland**
Date: Sunday, November 7, 1999

I have been stressing out about my Switzerland trip by myself at Christmas, especially since I have never seen a long distance train or train station here yet. Lisa called yesterday and asked if I wanted to go downtown to the ZOO train station (Bahnhof Berlin Zoologischer Garten) so she could explain it all to me. She got her railroad education riding trains to get to the ship for our cruise; I went via plane. I feel so much better now. She showed me how to find the platforms, how to find the car number, and how to look at the pictures to find the exact spot to stand for my reserved car to stop right infront of me. What a system!!!! *Gleis* is platform, that's mandatory to know.

When I decided Switzerland would be my Christmas Paradise this year, I walked into the travel agency and said I'd like to make reservations for Switzerland for Christmas. He said "All Full!" (at least he spoke English). I didn't let that deter me. I sat down and told him the dates I wanted to go and that I would be going by train, wanted a small mountain village in the Bernese Oberland Alps, and needed to be close enough to walk to the train station. He said "Hmmm..." and started looking through a catalog. Soon, he showed me the most beautiful picture of a Swiss village, nestled among many high mountains, and surrounded by TWO ski areas. I said "Yes!" and he made the arrangements.

Later I began to realize I didn't know how use the German long distance trains. I had learned how to travel by Swiss trains last year when I took my first overseas trip; a two week Swiss hiking trip in the French speaking area. I was with a group then and would not have learned the rail system except that I decided to go to the Matterhorn on our day off. The British guide took me to the tiny one-man train ticket window in our town of Les Diablerets, got me a train schedule booklet, and taught me how to read the thing. It's an amazingly organized system and a friend and I successfully made eight train changes that day to briefly gaze on the majestic Matterhorn above Zermat before rushing back to our hotel before its curfew closing.

When we finished at the train station, Lisa and I found a quaint café and had the best hot chocolate ever! It was served in a small bowl with a spoon and a huge topping of whipped cream. It was the sweetest hot chocolate and soooooooo hit the spot! Other times when I have ordered hot chocolate (*heiss schokolade*) here, it has been bitter, strong with chocolate, and void of sugar. Although we were probably supposed to eat it all with that spoon, we drank out of the bowl. Just Americans being Americans, I guess.

Energized from the bowl of hot chocolate, we strolled through the major shopping district of Berlin, window shopping in some of the most elegant and stylish shops until we realized we were lost. It was after 6 pm so everything was closed, but we found an information booth with a map. We needed to meet friends in two hours at a movie theater far away in area we'd never visited. Arriving early, we were thrilled to find an Irish Pub across from the theater, the first I've seen here. It was like the Irish Pubs in the United States (and maybe, Ireland???), and they spoke English!!!! We could read the menu; English was on the right and German on the left. Now I know where to go when I feel homesick.

From: Carol
To: LittleAli
Subject: **Sightings**
Date: Monday, November 8, 1999

I had dinner at Lisa's tonight, there were five of us. Two of them had seen Mikhail Gorbachev today. They went downtown and saw a little crowd of about 30 people gathering around a car. They went over, and there he was, getting out of the car to go into the best hotel here.

From: Carol
To: LittleAli
Subject: **Wall Celebration**
Date: Wednesday, November 10, 1999

The Wall Celebration was very exciting, inspiring, crowded and peaceful. Did you see it on TV? I just can't believe so many people can be so peaceful. The huge crowd stood in the rain (no seating available).

Germans do seem to be very good at self control and following rules. A German friend told me her culture doesn't have many jokes, but one she remembered was a picture of a huge crowd of protestors with no one on the grass because of a sign telling them to stay off the grass! I feel very safe here and haven't seen or heard any violence. I guess I wouldn't know if there were violent words, since I don't know the language yet. When I'm on the bus with a lot of teenagers, there are times I'm glad I don't know what they are saying. Somehow I sense I would be uncomfortable if I understood their conversations.

From: Carol
To: LittleAli
Subject: **Going to China**
Date: Thursday, November 11, 1999

Yesterday I went with friends to a travel agent. We reserved a trip to Beijing for our Winter Break in early February. Last weekend we went downtown Berlin to see a movie. Walking back underground through the tunnels to the U-Bahn (underground local train), we noticed a sign in the window of a closed Travel Agency. The tunnels are huge with shops along the sides. It was late, so most of the shops were closed. The sign said Peking and other German words which the seasoned travelers in my group said meant it was a great offer for a one week trip to Beijing, China in February including airfare, a 4-star hotel, and a guide to wonderful sites and events for only $500. All six of us wanted to go and now there are 10 in the group. It is China's off season, very cold, but at least it won't be so crowded with tourists. Their Chinese New Year celebration will be happening, and we're scheduled to visit the Great Wall of China too. With 10 in the group, we can get an English speaking tour guide instead of the German one that comes with the package.

Your Elderhostel trip to Bluff, Utah sounds educational and interesting, and I'm sure very beautiful. I love the wide open spaces of the Utah desert. I would have especially enjoyed hiking to American Indian archeology sites along the San Juan River. And Chimney Rock, Hovenweep and Arches National Park are really special places to visit, especially this time of year when it's cool.

From: Carol
To: LittleAli
Subject: **Faxed Article**
Date: Friday, November 12, 1999

Alice, thank you so much for faxing the ***Rocky Mountain News*** story of me to me. It's fun to have that connection with "back home" and actually be mentioned in a newspaper. There's so much history here, it's uplifting to be part of the celebrations.

From: Carol
To: LittleAli
Subject: **In Style Colors**
Date: Tuesday, November 16, 1999

It's been sooooooo cold here! Bitter cold! Today CNN said it might snow in Berlin today. It didn't. My theory is—it's just too cold to snow! That may be why Berlin never gets much snow. I've looked at the *Lands End* website and found just the Arctic coat I need! I'm letting my parents know that is my Christmas wish for this year.

You won't believe this, the clothing here only comes in three colors this winter! Every day on my way to work, I pass several nice clothing shops here in Zehlendorf. I've been surprised to see only black, dark gray, and a dull orangish-red on every mannequin in the window. One of my friends went in to shop and said all the clothes were that color. She asked why there weren't more colors and the sales clerk said they "weren't in style." So I guess I'm not in style, I wear other colors.

There are no zip lock bags here!!!! Or at least I can't find them. The only baggies have one twist tie per box. Do they expect me to recycle it through all the baggies? Oh my! I'm asking my parents to send some gallon and quart zip locks in the package with my coat. I'm also requesting the plastic grocery bags given out so freely at home; I like to use them for trashcan liners and to take out my trash. We don't get anything to put our groceries in here. Everyone carries cloth bags, a backpack, or the folding cart like I have. I know it's better for the environment, but in the meantime, I'm recycling the US ones here in the German trash.

From: Carol
To: LittleAli
Subject: **Teaching Teachers**
Date: Thursday, November 18, 1999

We had a training day for teachers, and I was the instructor! The goal was for all teachers to become comfortable using the school computers, to learn basic computer skills, and to begin recording their annual class goals in their individual computer file on our network. I had 35 teachers in the morning and 35 in the afternoon, for two days. About half the teachers are German, and half are English speaking, mostly American. All speak English well. Considering some had not used a computer and many were uncomfortable and even apprehensive, they did a great job and seemed thrilled with their accomplishments! I was very proud of them and I received many compliments and much praise from the teachers, the curriculum coordinator, and the principal. Being appreciated is such a high!

Since it will now be required that each teacher record their annual class goals in their computer file and keep them updated for access by administrators and other teachers, this training should be continuing success. So many times, people take computer classes but don't use the knowledge, so they forget what they've learned. I credit Steve, the curriculum coordinator/vice principal, for coming up with a plan to make computer use an on-going necessity.

From: Carol
To: LittleAli
Subject: **Early Thanksgiving**
Date: Sunday, November 21, 1999

About 30 of us got together this afternoon for our Thanksgiving in Germany Feast! It's a challenge to find ingredients, but we had a nearly authentic potluck Thanksgiving meal. I took coleslaw; we had a wonderful time and the food was great too.

I am just so impressed with the freshness of the produce! The vine fresh tomatoes smell just like they're in a summer garden. The only cucumbers are the long ones (English) but they're never bitter and always fresh. I haven't seen any cantaloupe but their Honeydew are always good. Eggs must be fresh because they are never refrigerated. I found that in Nepal, too, they didn't refrigerate their eggs and they did bring them on our 3-day trek!

We're all celebrating Thanksgiving early because school is dismissed Wednesday afternoon through Friday, giving us a nice long Thanksgiving break! We don't plan to stay here! Although America's Thanksgiving is not celebrated here, our school is Bilingual and Bicultural, so we celebrate all holidays of both countries, usually by not being in session.

Lisa and I are going to the Baltic Sea; we're staying on Rugen Island in a huge hotel in a little town called Binz.

It's in northern Germany, about five hours from here. The weather will be cold, but we just want to get away to a beautiful place, relax, read, and bundle up and walk on the rocky shore. This will be my first long distance train ride; I'll get to see much more of the old Eastern Germany. Russia is on the far eastern side of the Sea. Sweden and Denmark are on the northern shore, a four hour ferry ride from Germany.

Yesterday, coming back from buying the groceries, I fell on the sidewalk in the snow. The sidewalk was cobblestone and very uneven. A rocky part of the walk was sticking up and, not being able to see it under the thin cover of snow; I tripped and fell flat on the walk! Several people stopped to stare. It took me awhile to get my breath, dust off the snow, and awkwardly get to my feet. With so many watchers, I thought I should acknowledge them, so I said, in my best English, "I'm fine, thank you," and hobbled off. Today I'm a bit stiff, my back and right leg are hurting, but luckily I can walk; that's very important here. Without a car, I have to walk long distances every day.

From: Carol
To: LittleAli
Subject: **Baltic Sea**
Date: Tuesday, November 30, 1999

Lisa and I had a wonderful time at the Baltic Sea (Nord Sea). It was so relaxing and beautiful, and no colder than here. I enjoyed the long distance trains; they are very clean and comfortable.

We stayed at an elegant historic hotel in the small town of Binz on Rugen Island. The whole town is historic, everything is blue and white and very charming. I can picture the elite strolling along it's seaside promenade around the turn of the century, complete with women carrying parasols and wearing long dresses with bustles. Communication was a challenge; a woman at the hotel desk and one bus driver were the only English speaking people we met. My first stop was to purchase post cards of the places we wanted to visit. Those pictures and the information printed on them was our way of asking people for directions. Sometimes we had to walk long distances, then stand and wait for busses, but we found everything and the people were extremely helpful and kind.

One day we went on a Steam Train to an old castle named Jagdschloss Granitz. Just getting to the train station was a long walk, especially because we got lost a few times. The train ride was like going back in time and the castle was interesting. Its extremely narrow, very high staircase was the highlight. When we left the castle we learned the train had stopped running for the day. Someone called us a cab, and we went back inside to wait in the café. Taxis don't cost nearly as much here as in the United States; I don't know how many miles (kilometers) we were out of town.

Another day, we visited very picturesque Jasmund National Park and walked along the rocky shore and enjoyed the beautiful Chalk Cliffs. I loved being out in nature and far from the cities. Along the way we saw houses with grass roofs, farms, and lots of water. We walked about four miles a day, mostly through forests and along the water; sometimes in fields.

On the last day we went a long distance to the northern tip of the island. We had to change busses and learned that, unlike in Berlin; busses don't follow the posted schedules, and sometimes don't even stop at bus stops. We first realized this after waiting for our second bus about 20 minutes after it was scheduled to stop there. We walked into a nearby restaurant in a very remote area, and with hand signals and the few German words we knew, we got the message the bus would arrive in an hour. Luckily it was lunch time, so we enjoyed a delicious meal; the timing was perfect.

Our destination was a couple of lighthouses at the tip of the island. The weather was getting nasty, with wind and a very cold rain. As we were getting off the bus at the last stop, the bus driver spoke to us in English. He must have heard us talking. He said he'd be back to pick us up in two and a half hours and he pointed to the location where he would be stopping; not at the bus stop, of course. We were amazed he spoke English and so thankful he was watching out for us. He stressed it would be his last pick up of the day so we needed to be there.

The whole area was very remote, and by then, cold and windy. We had umbrellas but couldn't use them in the wind. Walking the long distances to the lighthouses was exhilarating!!! Visibility was near zero, so we couldn't see much from there. We were chilled and soaked to the bone, but as we came from the last lighthouse, a tiny café appeared in the middle of the field. Desperately needing something warm to drink, I pointed at the hot red drink everyone else was drinking and said "*ein, bitte*" they said "*mit?*" and I said "*ya.*" I figured whatever it was with, it would warm me more, and I wanted it. It turned out to be glühwein, a hot spiced wine which I really loved!!!! It was exactly what we needed for the walk back to the non-bus stop.

That wonderful bus driver (our Rugen Angel) was exactly where he said he would be when he said he'd be there. We sat right behind him for the long trip back to civilization.

He said he'd been traveling that route for 11 years and we were the first Americans he'd met. He had learned English as a child and seldom had a chance to practice. His English was very good and we never stopped talking for the rest of the trip. When we got to a small town, he said we'd need to switch to the train for Binz. It was dark by then, there was only one bus to get us home, he was finished with his shift, but he waited with us about 20 minutes until the next bus came. He walked with us to that bus and told the driver where we needed to go. Wow, can you imagine how impressed and relieved and thankful we were? Can you see why I call him our angel?

From: Carol
To: LittleAli
Subject: **Taxing Mail**
Date: Thursday, December 2, 1999

I'm such a slow learner! Thinking a $42 Lands End Fleece Jacket would be worth $42, and knowing anything valued less than $50 does not get taxed, I ordered the jacket. Well, that wasn't wise!

I went to the post office tonight to pick it up. The postage was $20, so the German government decided the package was valued at $62. Therefore, they charged me two separate 16% taxes, about $20. First they told me to pay 300 dm, which is about $150 and I said I didn't want it and turned to walk out. Then he said no, it was 37 marks, about $20. I paid it and took my package. What a hassle!

They did keep mentioning polyester (which the coat had in it). I got the distinct impression that was something they do tax extra, and they kept mentioning something about the ground, or dirt, or soil, but I didn't get any connection except it was a man-made fabric, not a natural one. Maybe my lack of understanding helped me get that coat at the discounted tax of only a mere $20. Wow, that jacket cost me $82, I hope it lasts a long time!*

My parents also just sent me the very warm coat I hinted I wanted for Christmas. The mail carrier delivered it to my door December 1st at 5 pm. Luckily, I was here and didn't have to pay extra. I had mother said it was valued at $30. She took off the tags so it would look used. This coat has a hood and lots of pockets, it's three quarter length and will keep me warm for the next two winters. There are many pockets; big ones, secret ones; I may not need a purse or suitcase for my travels!

Monday night about 15 of us met at TGI Fridays downtown Berlin for a November Birthday Celebration. We had a fun time and I treated myself to a decadent meal of Nachos and a Margarita. Nothing German about that!

Tuesday night I went to a pot luck the parents had for the teachers. It was really very nice and I loved talking with the parents. Sometimes I don't understand the German parents when they tell me their child's name, but they are patient with me. I am still amazed at how gracious the people here are. I've never felt so appreciated in my life.

Yesterday I had four friends over for chicken. No, I didn't cook it! There is a wonderful outdoor Turkish food stand featuring rotisserie chicken, .hanging pulled pork, and delicious salads on the way home from work. I picked up a chicken and salads. Great way to entertain! The actual purpose of the gathering was to figure out how to make Margaritas. They don't have Triple Sec or Margarita Salt here. We bought ingredients we thought might work and had a Margarita tasting party, what fun!!!. Lisa is having a big Jimmy Buffet Party Saturday night; what's a Jimmy Buffet Party without good Margaritas?

Christmas decorations are everywhere now. Without a Thanksgiving holiday, they begin decorating in early November. Everything is so beautiful, it lifts my spirits!

It's great you'll be spending Christmas in Salt Lake City with your daughter, her husband, and your new grandson! I'm sure they'll be happy to see you and may welcome some help with their little one.

---

* It's still in perfect shape in 2010.

From: Carol
To: LittleAli
Subject: **Dom Concert and Buffet Party**
Date: Monday, December 6, 1999

The concert at the beautiful Berliner Dom, a cathedral in downtown Berlin, was yesterday. Our school choirs and orchestra put on a delightful performance. Tears welled in my eyes throughout; the setting was spellbinding and I just couldn't get over the fact that I'm here!

Lisa had her Jimmy Buffet Party Saturday! What a party! I have no idea how many American and German teachers and administrators were there, dressed in island attire, wearing leis Lisa had shipped in from Hawaii. The small apartment was decorated with potted palm trees and fresh tropical blossoms. And the Margaritas were perfect!

From: Carol
To: LittleAli
Subject: **Alcohol Anywhere Anytime!**
Date: Wednesday, December 8, 1999

When the secretary told me I could put my sack lunch in the American and German principals' refrigerator, I was humorously surprised to have trouble finding space for my little sandwich amongst all the wine and champagne bottles. This place is so different from America!

A few weeks later, I was invited to a teacher's birthday party at lunch and was less surprised to be served wine. It was a nice party, we all enjoyed ourselves, and I imagine we all had a more relaxed afternoon teaching our classes. That is so different from back home where we would be fired for drinking wine in the workplace. Maybe we make too big a deal of it.

Today I was invited to a party in the hallway outside my classroom while I was teaching class. The teachers told me it was for a student teacher who was leaving. I said I couldn't come; I had a class to teach. In a few minutes, a German teacher was at my classroom door graciously handing me a glass of champagne and a piece of cake. Students didn't seem to think it at all unusual. I waited until after class, but that may not have been necessary. Bad behavior is never acceptable; people seem to act responsibly. I could get used to this!

From: Carol
To: LittleAli
Subject: **Nuremburg Magic**
Date: Monday, December 13, 1999

Eight of us hopped a train and went to the 1000 year old city of Nuremburg for the weekend. I've never traveled so light; I only took a backpack! I carried it to work Friday, then on to the bus and S-Bahn and the long distance train. It was a beautiful journey through the German countryside. Even after dark, the distant farm lights were nostalgic.

This is the most beautiful city I've ever seen. It's mostly Medieval, with a castle just outside of the city, a wall around the city, and three magnificent cathedrals right near the Market Square. The buildings are old world architecture with Art Nouveau style paintings on the buildings. It seemed small; we were able to walk everywhere, sometimes over the river on graceful arched brick bridges. The Christmas Market was what we came for and where we spent our days. This is said to be the biggest and best Christkindlesmarkt in Germany, and I do believe it! I loved looking at all the crafts and festive displays, but my favorites were the Lebkuchen (a delicious type of decorated gingerbread cookie), the little Nuremburg sausages, and the Glühwein (remember the hot spiced wine from Rugen? I found it again!!! It's my new favorite winter drink!). Somehow sipping on glühwein as I walk around the market makes it all so relaxing and even magical.

My favorite memory was being the only person in a magnificent cathedral early Sunday morning. I had my special time for prayer and inspiration before someone came to light the candles and I left for my day at the market. My favorite restaurant was in a huge ancient castle-like stone building full of tunnels and hidden rooms. The food was very heavy, mostly pork and potatoes; I chose stuffed cabbage with minced lamb, a special kind of potato salad, and lots of sausages and sauerkraut. Everything was delicious and so old world.

I now have Christmas gifts to send home; now the challenge will be packaging and getting them mailed. I hope they don't have to go through customs as they leave or at home.

From: Carol
To: LittleAli
Subject: **More Mail Stories**
Date: Thursday, December 16, 1999

My Aunt Jean sent me a Christmas Package through UPS straight from an almond company. Last Wednesday I received a note on my door that UPS had a package for me. It was in German and I couldn't read it, but I called their office Thursday and they agreed to deliver it Friday. Since someone had to sign, they agreed to bring it to my workplace between 11 and 1, and a secretary could sign for it. I alerted the secretaries and checked for it Friday, Monday, Tuesday—no package! On Wednesday, I called UPS again. They said they had delivered a package, maybe mine, maybe not, to someone in my building named Samland. Great record keeping!

I went to a neighbor named Samland (name is on the door) and had my students write in German for me, "I am your neighbor, do you have a package for Carol Coffey?" When she opened the door, she did speak English, I introduced myself, and she immediately said she had a package for me. I was very thankful, but am left wondering—why didn't

UPS leave a note on my door saying it was with Samland; why didn't UPS know whose package was handed over to Samland?

This evening I went over to Lisa's (she's in another building) and when I came back, a neighbor I don't know stopped me at the street and said she had two packages for me. She said I could come to her apartment at 10 pm tonight. That is so sweet that people here are taking care of me. It is better than making the trip to the post offices or downtown to customs. As safe as this place seems, I would really prefer they just leave it at the door.

UPS is no better in the United States. In 1996, they left my new computer, monitor, and printer on the steps of my condo. People have stolen things from porches there, but luckily mine was safe that time. When I lived in Divide, UPS couldn't even get to me on my muddy roads. They were trying to deliver my passport just before the trip to Nepal in May and I had to tell the Travel Agent to just send it by regular mail, which went to my post office box in town. Even overnight postal service or FedEx could not get to me. So I should not be complaining about mail service here.

Erin is traveling from Connecticut to visit my parents in West Virginia tonight. I am hoping she will call me in the middle of the night from there. I'm anxious to hear about the trip and the visit. From there she will be driving back to college in St Louis. Her internship is over; her last semester of college will soon begin.

From: Carol
To: LittleAli
Subject: **Swiss Fairy Tale**
Date: Wednesday, December 29, 1999

I had an amazing Christmas Vacation. Departing Sunday, December 19th on a long distance train, I had a beautiful trip, only two train changes, and all went nearly as scheduled, arriving only one hour late. White Christmas lights flickered from homes and farms scattered throughout the countryside. I haven't seen colored lights anywhere yet; I'm thinking they are not used here.

Kandersteg is in a valley totally surrounded by beautiful majestic peaks. Snow is everywhere, on streets, sidewalks, trees, roof tops, and of course on the ground and the mountains. People pull their groceries home on little sleds. The postman pulls larger sleds through the streets on foot. Walking past some homes, I smelled the distinct fragrance of cattle wintering in the lower level or in the building attached at the side of the house. It was raining hard when I got there last Sunday night. It was hard for me to realize it was raining on snow, as it never does in Colorado. Luckily, the snow stayed and the rest of the week was beautiful until Christmas day when it rained all day with blizzards in the high mountains. Chair lifts at the two ski areas here were closed; too much wind. Christmas day was the only day I had time to read a book. I enjoyed being cozy inside, reading and having lunch in the hotel restaurant. Breakfast and dinner was included with the package, but lunch was always elsewhere on my own.

With my Swiss Rail Pass, I could travel anywhere without extra fees. One day I went to Grindelwald and took a cog train up to the Jungfraujoch, near the top of a mountain. The train was inside the mountain most of the time, with a few stops to get out and view ice sculptures inside the tunnel and peer through windows at the mountains outside. At the top, we exited into a building. The upper level was a restaurant with incredible views of the Bernese Oberland Alps in all directions, with the well known Eiger, Monch, and Jungfrau peaks right there. The Swiss really know how to civilize the mountains!

That whole trip was extremely spectacular; way more beautiful than I ever imagined. On the train to Grindelwald I met a young couple from Tasmania. Since they spoke English, we found a lot to talk about. They were sledding on the ski slopes for the day, riding the train like we'd ride a chair lift or gondola; skiers were also riding the train. They told me other places they'd been on this vacation, giving me ideas of more places to visit next time. Surprisingly, when I arrived back in Grindelwald from my excursions, they had just arrived from their day on the slopes, so we rode back down the valley together, sharing stories of an exhilarating day in the Alps. I also met a young couple from New York on that trip. They are the only people from the U. S. I've seen the whole week.

When I departed the train in Kandersteg that evening, the most amazing surprise was awaiting me! It was the night of the full moon, but not just any full moon. I learned the following day on BBC that it was the brightest and biggest full moon ever—because of its distance from Sun to Earth, Sun to Moon, and Moon to Earth, I think. How lucky am I? I got to see this amazing phenomenon in the Swiss Alps—three times!!! When I got off the train, there it was, just rising over the mountains. I stopped and stared, I just could not believe how big and bright it was, lighting up the mountains like daylight on this clear crisp night. As I walked into town (closer to the mountains) the moon was not visible anymore. I noticed a group of people ahead at the corner. They were waiting for the moon to rise. I stood with them and watched it rise over the mountains again, just as startlingly big and bright as before! When I turned to walk to my hotel (closer to the mountains), the moon disappeared again. But when I got to the hotel, I waited for it to rise again, to soak in the splendor of the moment; to remember forever. That whole night was so bright I kept waking and looking out my window at the mountains, the snow, the moon, and the glistening "moon diamonds" in the snow—reflections from the moon. Sleep could wait for another night; this night was too precious to miss.

One day I rode the train down the valley to the town of Thun, walked up a long steep hill to visit a castle, and just enjoyed walking around this medieval town. The shopping area and much of the city was on an island. I walked across ancient covered bridges spanning the rivers. It was a trip back in time; an out of this world feeling.

Another day trip took me to the tiny mountain village of Zermatt. It is in a different direction from my other train rides. This is really strange; the train goes all the way through the mountain from Kandersteg. The road ends in Kandersteg and cars get on the train to continue through the mountain tunnel. The Swiss are still amazing me with their innovative transportation.

The sky was blue, the air was clear, and the magnificent Matterhorn was in full view! I understand it's usually cloudy in the summer, as it was when I visited it summer before last. What a spectacular sight, standing so proud and apart from the other peaks! I rode the Gornergrat Bahn (cog railway) above Zermatt to get continual Matterhorn (14,690 ft) views and spectacular views of Monte Rosa (15,000+ ft) and other peaks from the top. Passenger cars are not allowed in Zermatt, but goats and people are free to roam the quaint streets. I found Matterhorn posters for my classroom and apartment; for beauty and the memories.*

When I had extra time I walked around Kandersteg, hiked on snow-packed trails, and rode a chairlift to the ski slopes and ski warming hut where I enjoyed lunch or just a glass of wine in the afternoon outside at a picnic table in the snow with mountain peaks all around. Life just can't get any better! At the ski area, I walked on snow packed by sledders (little sleds are for rent) pulling sleds back to sledding slopes. In Colorado, if you try to walk on a ski slope, you sink in and leave sitzmarks, but the Swiss snow is more moist and packs nicely for hikers, sledders, and skiers to enjoy. After hiking about a mile, I came to a frozen lake surrounded by elegant spruce trees with a mountain backdrop, like a scene in a fairy tale! Although two ski areas are here, the other one wasn't scheduled to open until December 25th.

On the shortest day of the year, I rode the chairlift before sunlight appeared in the valley and was enjoying lunch on the slope as that lazy sun finally rose high enough to light the valley at 12:45 pm! The valley is deep, it doesn't get dark until 5:15 pm (in Berlin it is totally dark at 4 pm now) but I watched the sunlight leave the valley floor at 3:15 pm that day. It was intriguing and mesmerizing to watch the shadows move across the valley and the mountains.

My hotel, Alfa-Soleil, was elegant, charming, and old; with a beautiful ceramic tile underground swimming pool, sauna, exercise room and solarium. The decorations were natural and tasteful; the restaurant, bar, and inviting lounge areas were all decorated with Christmas décor and white lights. My room was tiny, clean, and basic with just a single bed, bathroom, TV, phone, little desk, and a closet. My view was incredible and my windows opened wide; I love the fresh winter air! The $300 total I paid for the room and meals is such a bargain! I am so glad single rooms are common in Europe; it keeps the price down for me to be able to travel alone. When I travel at home, I have to get a double room, so I'm paying for two, and can't afford that very often.

The food was elegant and included many courses, gracious service, creative presentations, and a great variety of delicious foods. I sat alone at a small table the first two nights (they assign you a table by your room number) but Tuesday they had a fondue and put people together. I was put with the three other single English-speaking women, who were from London. We enjoyed being together and requested we be seated together from then on.

Christmas Eve, we also requested another English couple sit with us, so there were six at our table for the three hour dinner/Christmas program. After dinner, we walked to the Protestant (Reform) church for a 10:30 service. This beautiful very small old wooden church was filled when we got there, so they sent us up steep narrow stairs to the miniscule balcony. Thankfully, I seem to have conquered my claustrophobia, and was able to enjoy the service. Although German is the language spoken in this part of Switzerland, the program was presented in four languages. The large live Christmas tree decorated only with real lighted white candles did make me a bit nervous, but I decided this church had been around for a couple of centuries at least, probably with candles on live trees every year, so they must know how to pull it off safely. We had song sheets printed in four languages and we all sang the familiar carols in our own language; it brought tears to my eyes and a lump in my throat to be there on that magical Christmas Eve singing the same songs in many tongues.

On Christmas Day in Kandersteg, there is a tradition that young men from 17-20 years of age put on incredible costumes and visit homes and establishment throughout the day. People must let them in, or it would be bad luck. Hosts provide drink and goodies, so by the end of the day, the boys are quite playful. While I was having lunch, the "Christmas creatures" called *Pelzmartiga* came into the hotel. There was a "Green Monster," a "Fur Man" dressed in a variety of natural furs, a "Quilt Man" dressed in quilt pieces, a "Card Player" dressed in playing cards all over his outfit, and a "Pine Tree" covered in pine boughs. The costumes are quite old and need to be refurbished each year. Traditionally, they force out the evil spirits on Christmas Day; then return New Years' Day to protect the house and insure evil spirits can not get in for the coming year.

On Christmas Day, I was able to call my parents, and my daughters who are visiting their dad in Colorado. It sounded like everyone was having a good holiday and it was great to talk to them all in the daytime!

My train trip back to Berlin began December 26. I have much to say about that, so it will come in the next email.

Happy New Year!

---

*I still have two of the Matterhorn posters hanging on my walls in 2010.

From: Carol
To: LittleAli
Subject: **Train Story**
Date: Thursday, December 30, 1999

I left Kandersteg, Switzerland at 9:30 am December 26, 1999 in some light rain with snow still everywhere. The hotel van took me and three of my new British friends to the train station five minutes away. Two of the women were just going to Bern for the day. The other one (Marilyn) was heading home to London. The train didn't stay on schedule, it actually stopped twice briefly for no apparent reason, and by the time we got to Bern, Marilyn had missed her eight minute connection to the next train. That meant I had missed my 11 minute one for later in the afternoon in Mannheim, too; but I wasn't worried. I knew there was one an hour later there, and that was the only place I had to change trains, so I felt all safe, secure, and ready for a relaxing trip. It was raining very hard in Bern, and there seemed to be some wind, but I didn't think much about it, except for hoping the rain would stop so Kate and Elizabeth would have a better day there.

Just out of Bern, the train got slower and slower, sometimes stopping for no reason again. At some little town I couldn't find on my map, we were told the train couldn't go any further; that no trains were running because the storm had damaged the electric lines the trains run on, and we would need to get out and get a bus to Olton. We got out at a little train station and waited for an hour in very hard rain and wind for a bus that never came. That's probably good. We were under a huge shelter, but the rain and wind still got to us.

The trains started running again, and we were able to get on one that was supposed to take us to Olton where we would need to change for the trip north. That train stopped in every little town, but the sun came out, the rain stopped, and things looked pretty good. We got to Olton after an hour or more (should have been 15 minutes). We were able to get on a train headed north.

That's when we began to notice trees down and other wind damage. When we got to Basel, on the Swiss/German border, a big section of the train station roof had collapsed. We were told to get out and that no trains were going into Germany at all. They didn't know when or if they would. Luckily I was sitting by a wonderful young Swiss girl whose Grandmother lived in Basel, so she knew the town well. She gave me a walking tour of the city, we had lunch, and visited a beautiful Cathedral, saw the Rhine River, and also saw much wind damage. Many trees and Christmas decorations were down, windows had been broken, and some streets were barricaded. The weather was good then with just a few gusts of wind, no rain, and a little sunshine. Three hours later, we went back to the station and were told no trains were running from there but they thought if we took a tram to the German side of town, the train station there many be able to get us into Germany. Getting the luggage from our locker, we took the tram, and got to the German station.

They said a train was headed north to Mannheim and Hamburg in five minutes—so we RAN and made it! About 20 minutes later, the train took off. We saw lots more wind damage along the way, and had some mysterious stops. In a very short time, we stopped at Freiburg and were told the train would need to wait 30 minutes because there was only one track cleared and we were third in line. After waiting there for two hours, they announced it would be at least another hour wait; no trains may be able to go all night. They even suggested we should get off and check into a hotel. I didn't care which we did, so my Swiss friend (Sandra) said she needed five minutes to decide what to do. She really needed to be back at work that day, and had been using her cell phone to contact colleagues and organizing them in case she didn't make it. I went to the toilet but didn't mention where I was going. Two minutes later, with no warning at all, the train took off! Sandra was quite concerned I might have stepped off the train a moment and there she was with my luggage, but I was on the train and when I got back to the seat, we settled in for the trip north again.

Soon they announced people going to Berlin should get off at a small place before Mannheim to take a train to Berlin. But before we got there, they announced we should get off at Mannheim (as my ticket said) to get a train to Berlin. But just before Mannheim they announced we would change farther along at Frankfurt. Sandra got off in Mannheim to go to Bonn; we exchanged email addresses.

Just before Frankfurt they announced we would get off at a tiny place called Fulda and a special train would come in to take us to Berlin. When we got to Fulda, they made us get off, the place was deserted and nothing was open. It was 12:30 am and there was no indication of any trains there all night. We stood out in the dark in the cold and rain where they told us to stand, not even knowing which platform to be on, and waited very skeptically. I will admit, I had a few thoughts of Nazi Germany and people being forced to ride trains to concentration camps. As you can imagine, a couple of people were getting mad and one man was yelling to the conductor. It's probably good he did, because our train stayed there and in 10 minutes we heard an announcement that a train would be leaving for Berlin on Platform 6 in five minutes—well, guess what, the train we came in on was still there—on Platform 6!!!!!!!!! And that was the train we had to get on (back on!) Boy, were they confused, but I'm really glad they didn't leave us in tiny Fulda, as it would have been all night outside in the cold with no shelter or facilities and I'm sure, no train.

As we were riding along in the same train, they announced those going to Berlin should get out at Hannover and get a train for Berlin. That made more sense, as that was directly west of Berlin and would be the closest place on this northern route, and Hannover is a bigger city. At 3:10 am about 100 of us got off at Hannover. We rushed to the information desk; they didn't know we were coming. They didn't have a train to Berlin. We waited, a couple of people yelled things but I didn't know what they said. Then the police came and all was calm. Soon they announced a train was coming from Munich to Berlin and would swing over and pick us up. Actually the train arrived very soon, we rushed to the platform. Can you imagine 100 people running together from place to place? It was crazy! They had us wait until they attached two more cars for us. By then I had another friend. I was the only non German speaking person and certainly the only American on the whole train. Luckily I was able to find kind helpful people who could interpret for me. Several people were watching out for me. This time my new friend was a young German man, a Social Worker in Berlin. He had chosen the Buddhist way of life, had trekked in Tibet and Nepal, and was going to India the next week to walk around a holy mountain and be with his Buddhist teacher who was preparing to die. When I was in Nepal in May, our Nepalese Guide told us most Nepalese people are both Buddhist and Hindu. Hindu is their religion; Buddhism is their way of life. The Tibetans, however, practice only Buddhism.

My newest Guardian Angel explained he would quickly jump on the train and save me the first seat possible. My one small suitcase was heavy, but I got on pretty fast and found the seat he was saving for me. Later he made sure I got off at the closest place to my apartment (Wannsee); no announcements were made and I didn't know we were even in Berlin yet. If I had gone on the Zoo station, it would have taken me 45 minutes longer and lots more taxi fare to get home. I was so grateful.

Five of us sat upright on bench seats facing each other in our cramped compartment. Our bags were overhead. I slept from 3:30 am till 6:15 am when I got off—13 hours later than scheduled. I did actually sleep without leaning on anything or anyone or letting my head nod. I think that comes from doing meditation and it's been a convenient method to get needed sleep in confined conditions.

I'm so grateful for all the gracious helpful people I met. Most people were very patient, relaxed and in a good mood. They kept telling me this was very uncommon and that their trains usually run on schedule. We heard this was a terrible storm, 50 people had been killed from falling trees etc., but we felt safe the whole time. The only real concerns seemed to be for those who would be late to work. Thankfully my Buddhist friend was able to get to work on time. He had to get a man out of jail that day. It was his client's court date and only chance to get out of jail for many months, and my friend was leaving in one week for that 6-month trip.

I never felt frustrated; I was relaxed throughout, and really didn't mind all the inconveniences. Since I didn't have to go to work for a week, I had no problems. No one was worrying about me; it was good to be free of the "strings".

I'm sure this will go down as one of my good memories because of the people.

The next day I heard the storm was very bad in France, especially in Paris, people were without electricity, trains were not running, and 60 people had died from the storm. They said the wind was 254 km in Switzerland and that Hurricane force was 140 km I think. It was supposedly one of Europe's worst storms.

I slept until noon that day and Lisa called and had me over for lunch. She made homemade Lasagna. It had taken her awhile to find a place to buy Ricotta cheese and the noodles, so this was the first time she had made Lasagna. It was excellent; she's such a great cook! Then we watched *Grumpy Old Men.*

I'm so thankful for wonderful people in my life.

From: Carol
To: LittleAli
Subject: **A New Year**
Date: Sunday, January 2, 2000

Well, my computer works! The world didn't end and the computers didn't crash in this New Year and New Millennium; that's a relief!

For New Year's Eve, I stayed here. I don't like crowds and I wanted to be reflective, contemplative, insightful, set goals, make resolutions, and have a very quiet evening. That didn't happen! People started setting off fireworks at dusk and kept it up till dawn! Non-stop! All kinds! Right here at my apartment building, in the yard, on the sidewalks, and in the street! It was like a war zone. I don't understand the fascination; it seems it would be a reminder of bombs during the war. I felt especially sorry for people trying to drive cars on the normally very busy street here. Traffic was light; the street was full of fireworks; sometimes firecrackers went off right in front of a moving car. Some fireworks were the beautiful very high ones, going well above my 4-story building. I sure missed the controlled, safe displays we have in the U. S.

Some friends went to the Brandenburg Gate downtown for the festivities. The big show went off at midnight, but many individuals had their own and set them off in the crowds all evening. The crowds were so tight, a couple of my small female friends were knocked down, but the guys with them were able to get them up again. It was televised and they said two million people were there.

Lisa had a brunch for several of us on New Years' Day, including guests from Malta, Cologne, London, and Susan and Kevin's son* from the U. S. It was a very interesting group with fascinating stories of a variety of Christmas vacation experiences.

Krysta was in a bad car accident but came out of it with only scratches on her arm. The car hit a cement barrier and rolled over at least once. Her shoes were her first concern; they were thrown from the car. She must have had Divine Protection. I am very thankful she is ok, but will continue to worry about her; it's a mother's prerogative.

I got a permanent this afternoon and it actually looks good! The hairdresser gave me the best hair cut I've ever had. The cut took about 45 minutes and he had me leaning over forwards, then standing up to make sure it hangs right from every angle. He was recommended by many teachers at my school, I can see why.

I am looking forward to going back to work Tuesday; it's been a very long holiday.

---

*Several years later, their son is living in Berlin with his new wife and working at JFKS, following in his parents' footsteps all around the world.

From: Carol
To: LittleAli
Subject: **Erin's Graduation Tickets**
Date: Tue, January 4, 2000

I just reserved my flight to St Louis for Erin's May Graduation from Webster College! I'm so excited! My parents are going to drive from West Virginia, too. I will miss three days' pay at work, but I gotta go! How could I miss my daughter's graduation?

Get this: The airline can't send the ticket here; they have to be mailed to an address in the United States. I am asking my parents to accept it there and send it registered mail to me. Gosh, I do hope that works! I guess I could have gone to a travel agent here and worked through them to get it mailed here, but I bet me doing it directly is cheaper—especially since I get to use my air miles. American Airlines delayed our group two days on our Switzerland trip in 1998; consequently they gave us 30,000 air miles for our shortened Swiss trip.

The sun was out today and the sky looked somewhat blue part of the time. What a welcome sight! We've had a very bleak winter, with gray skies that blend into the buildings so it's hard to separate them.

I didn't send Christmas packages till this week, and I received a Christmas package from my sister Mary today. I think I want to call off gift giving next year; the cost of postage just makes it ridiculous.

From: Carol
To: LittleAli
Subject: **Northern Exposure Party**
Date: Tue, January 25, 2000

I had a Northern Exposure Party in my little apartment tonight—25 people made it a cozy affair. I called it a picnic, had rotisserie chicken and salad, we sat on pillows on the floor or anything we could find to sit on. Since our days are so short, and winter so long, we got together to watch the Northern Exposure episode where they have 24 hours of darkness at Winter Solstice. It seemed relevant to our life here, but much worse, so I thought it would cheer us up. As you know, Northern Exposure is my favorite, so I ordered videos of all (6) of the episodes Amazon.com had. Postage made it expensive, but it's immensely valuable for my psyche.

It was a good mix of people including some of our German friends and some Americans we don't often see. I had said to come early, eat from 5-6, movie from 6-7 and promised an early evening. They left by 9. Some brought flowers (tulips and yellow roses) so my place looks and smells great. I told them not to bring anything but some brought food anyway. Ellen brought Baked Alaska, it was a big hit! I've had many compliments about the party and the mix of people; I believe they sincerely had fun. I know I did.

From: Carol
To: LittleAli
Subject: **No China Trip**
Date: Wed, January 26, 2000

Well, I'm not going to China next Monday after all. Monday I couldn't walk very well when I started out to go to work. My right foot wouldn't bend much, so I hobbled long very slowly. I thought it would go away soon; the muscles in my feet have been cramping recently but it would go away in a few blocks. This time there's a very sore spot on top of my foot near the toes, it's swollen and very tender. It didn't get better, so I took off work today and went to an orthopedic doctor. He couldn't give me an immediate fix. I was hoping for a cortisone shot or something fast and easy, but he said we needed to get to the root of the problem. My whole right side is messed up, it's hasn't felt right since I fell right before Thanksgiving. I have pain in the leg, back, shoulder, neck, and hip. The spine is crooked and my muscles are battling each other in all directions.

The doctor is prescribing several types of treatment: heat, massage, new orthotics for my shoes, and a visit to an Internist who specializes in Rheumatism and Arthritis. I'm to take blood tests and be checked over there. He thinks something is wrong internally and wants to check that out. I just hope it can be fixed fast!

I tried to explain how I needed to go to China Monday and walk on the Great Wall, but he said "No Way!" I guess he's right; I wouldn't be able to keep up with the group, lift a suitcase, or walk very far. Today I hobbled down to the Travel Agent and cancelled. Since I didn't have Travel Insurance, I am losing 60% of my money; I'm actually surprised I didn't lose it all.

I have learned a lesson: I will be purchasing Travel Insurance for all future trips! Insurance is very inexpensive and could be a big help if needed. When I broke my ankle attempting to paraglide in the Swiss Alps, my travel insurance took care of my medical expenses. Surprisingly, it didn't cost much, but it was good to get reimbursed after the trip.

At our Orientation, we had to choose our health insurance. We could choose the Public Insurance, which was less expensive, most Germans use it, but it would not pay when we were outside of Germany. Knowing I would be traveling, I chose the Private Insurance. The drawback to Private was that it was more expensive (but not as much as in the U. S.) and they would not pay for preexisting conditions. Since I didn't know of any preexisting conditions, it wasn't a problem. Now I know I could have used Travel Insurance and had the Public Insurance, too.

The doctor did say I should stay off my feet for two weeks, rest a lot, and not go to work. But I said I was OK in the classroom, the hard part was just getting to work. He didn't "write me out" as they do here. If I change my mind, I should let him know. I'll go in tomorrow and see. Since we have next week off for Winter Break, I may not need to miss much work. Healing and being able to walk well is my goal, so I'll do whatever is needed. I have lots of appointments and treatments scheduled; that might make it very hard to go to work too. I walk very slowly with small steps since my toes don't bend well. Otherwise, life is good, and I'm still having an adventure.

From: Carol
To: LittleAli
Subject: **Health Care**
Date: Sat, January 29, 2000

As you know, I declined the doctor's suggestion of writing me out of work for two weeks. I determinedly went to work Thursday, but my foot got so bad that evening I almost couldn't walk home from the last bus stop. Friday morning, I was in so much pain, I called in sick. We don't get sick days here without a written doctor's permission, so I called the doctor and he wrote me out for two weeks! So much for trying to tough it out!

We Americans traditionally go to work when we're sick or injured. Germans just don't have that philosophy. They believe in taking care of themselves as the highest priority. My employers here don't want us to come to work if we are sick or injured, but we must get to a doctor and he will write us out of work for a period of time much longer than I would ever think was necessary. It is probably much healthier and probably even heightens productivity, not to mention making for a healthier population.

Since I've been written out for two weeks, I cannot go back to work earlier. I will only miss a week of work because Winter Break lasts for one week. And if I do go back to work early, I will not receive any pay for those days!!!!! How's that for enforcing doctors' orders?

I soaked my foot in hot water, put Capsaicin Cream on it, and a sock over it. That felt good and was much better by 2 pm when I was able to get to the Grocery Store. I do have friends who were planning to do that for me, but you know how I like to "do it myself." When I got home, the doctor's office called to say my orthotics were ready. I was surprised it had only taken two days; I went downtown on busses and trains with very little walking.

I'm so impressed! The orthotics take the pressure off the part of the bottom of the foot that's tender and put pressure in my arch and other places. I can actually walk without much pain if I take little steps. They are much softer than the ones I've worn at home. I have worn orthotics off and on for the past 10 years. These cover the length of the foot and replace the shoe's regular insole. At home they just cover ¾ the length and must be worn on top of the shoe's regular insole. Luckily I was wearing boots I bought here. I was shocked when they reached into my boot and took out the insole! I had no idea they were made for that. The orthotics fit right in, how amazing is that? I have needed that kind of shoe for years but couldn't find it in the U. S.

It turns out there are shoe stores here that have a big variety of regular looking shoes which all have replaceable insoles; special stores just for me! Looks like I'll be shoe shopping soon.

I've gone for two massages and heat treatments. The massage is to try to straighten my spine and relax the tight muscles that are pulling my whole right side. The heat treatments are wonderful and feel so good! Huge gel filled soft heating pads are heated in water; then put on my sore areas. Each one covers about ¼ of my body and stays warm for the 20 minute treatment. Luckily the treatments are at a physical therapy complex within walking distance. I love these natural non-invasive treatments. After six treatments, I go back to the Orthopedic Doctor to review my status.

While I'm sitting around healing, I plan to study the German Language! I haven't been very successful yet. I have the excuse of my old age, but I don't have the excuse of "not enough time" now.

When my friends found out I was not going to China, they came with American videos to keep me entertained. They brought 20 videos of American TV shows and movies. So sweet!

I have been using ibuprophen for my foot and the general pain I've been having. It is not used much here; they don't have any coated ones to protect the stomach and is very expensive; so Mother has been sending coated Advil in my care packages. I am very thankful.

My parents just drove to Atlanta in an ice storm to visit my sister, then and on to Florida to visit other relatives. Luckily they are home safely now and enjoyed their trip.

From: Carol
To: LittleAli
Subject: **Banking Bliss**
Date: Wed, February 2, 2000

After a visit to the bank today, I realized I've actually grown to love this banking system. Instead of writing checks, we fill out a little form with our KontoNummer (bank number I guess) and the KontoNummer of the person or business we want to pay, name of the business, the date, and the amount in numerals. We slip the form into the bank slot or take it inside. Anytime we want an up-to-date statement, we go to a machine in the entry of the bank, which is never locked. We put in our EC card (which they provided) and get our up-to-date statement. We can also get cash with the EC card there free of charge. You can do it every day, anytime. So I don't need to have my own record book, I just staple my statements together about once a month. This probably only works if you have a nice cushion of money, which, luckily, I do. Since I don't have to pay taxes the first two years, I don't need a record of anything; such freedom! That EC card is a debit card with our picture for positive identification. It seems to work in all the machines everywhere in Europe.

From: Carol
To: LittleAli
Subject: **Mud and Answering Machines**
Date: Fri, February 4, 2000

I went for a Mud Treatment, a Heat Treatment, and Massage Therapy today! Mud was first—and real!!! What a mess! They had me on a cart right beside a shower. I was covered in mud and able to slide into the shower to clean off afterwards. The Heat treatment was next; Massage came last! I have declined all future mud treatments. The others were wonderful and very welcome.

I have been frustrated to find that most businesses do not use answering machines. They often do not answer the phone, so I have to just keep trying until they're ready to pick up. It certainly is challenging to make doctor and treatment appointments, which I am having a least once a day now. I'm practicing patience in this relaxed culture.

From: Carol
To: LittleAli
Subject: **Cultural Comparisons**
Date: Sat, February 5, 2000

Since I have a relaxed weekend at home, no treatments, and no trips; I think this is a good time to just mention some of the cultural differences I've been noticing. It is a different life here; I am adjusting to some of the changes and happily embracing others.

I'm learning more about fashion; every woman must have black boots and a long black wool coat, with a warm scarf of course. All winter, all women wear long black wool coats, usually with gray wool scarves. The scarves are all folded in half lengthwise, placed around the neck with ends meeting the fold in front, and pulling the ends through the fold just so.

I am very lucky! An American teacher who has been here a year went on a diet and lost so much weight she couldn't wear her standard black wool coat. Since I sadly am the weight she used to be, she graciously gave me her coat! It's in perfect condition and of excellent quality, and she wouldn't let me pay her anything! I bought a new gray wool scarf to go with my beautiful black wool coat and black boots (even my underwear is black)! Now I fit in!

The trash system here is very efficient. When you see one trash can, look farther, there are always three trash cans of different colors; one for paper, one for cans; one for everything else except glass. Glass disposal units are located somewhere in each neighborhood. Grocery stores also have glass vending machines; people stand in line to put their glass bottles into a machine which rewards them with money.

This is a bicycle-riding culture. It's wonderful to see so many people riding anywhere and everywhere. People of all ages, in all kinds of weather, are pedaling all over the city and suburbs. They have their own special "bike path" which runs alongside the sidewalk between the walk and the street. There is a strip of grass between the bike path and walk. It's a good thing everyone is required to have liability insurance. If I get hit by a bicycle while in or crossing a bike path, it is my fault and I am liable. When crossing the street, we must first look both ways before we cross the bike path; then look both ways before crossing the street. Bikes are not allowed on busses, but they can be taken on the trains with a special ticket.

Train and bus tickets are mandatory but seldom checked. People are trusted to always have the proper ticket, but they are only randomly checked. I have never been checked but have always had the proper ticket. I like this system, it gives the feeling that we're being trusted to do the right thing, and I'm convinced that most people do.

Dogs are everywhere—on buses, trains, restaurants, grocery stores, department stores, etc. I've heard dogs are required to take dog training classes. Always on a lease, they are extremely well behaved, and don't sniff or jump up to greet strangers. Their owners obviously take very good care of them and are proud of their canine families.

Children are also cared for very well here. Fresh air is so important; parents bring the children out in all weather. I've seen strollers rigged with rain gear to keep the little ones dry and warm but still let in that precious fresh air. All year, all our students are required to go outside to play at recess unless it's raining hard. Snow is not a problem; neither are frigid temperatures. Parents believe daily fresh air and exercise are important for good health. Since I am a self professed Fresh Air Fanatic, I've found my niche!

Most students and people of all ages wear neck scarves on cold days. High windows are open from the top in school and most buildings and apartments. Children are taught not to sit in drafts, and to use their neck scarves outside and inside when they are cold or feel a draft. I think this is a great idea, Lots of Fresh Air but Beware of Drafts! My Principal opens my window from the top every morning before I arrive; it's just too high for me to reach.

From: Carol
To: LittleAli
Subject: **Back from China**
Date: Sun, February 6, 2000

The group got back from China Friday night (Feb 4) at 6:30 pm. They were very tired from the long plane ride, but had a wonderful time, saying it was beautiful and "out of this world." Their English speaking guide was terrific and accompanied them everywhere.

I am so concentrated on healing, and so busy going to doctors, treatments, and therapies; I haven't felt bad about missing out on that adventure. Lisa and Amy came bearing gifts from the Orient today. They are so sweet.

From: Carol
To: LittleAli
Subject: **Lost Therapist**
Date: Wed, February 9, 2000

I got lost yesterday! I've been going to so many different places for treatments, I began to feel confident that I could pick up the subway and bus maps and find my way with only an address and no special instructions. Wrong! Today I got off the bus on the right street, but on the wrong end of that very long street! After walking at least 20 blocks on my physically challenged feet and legs, I arrived at the building of my new physical therapist's office 15 minutes late.

Exhausted but determined, I proceeded to slowly climb four flights of stairs! Berlin has very few elevators. People stay in shape walking numerous flights of steps to their apartments, in S-Bahn and train stations, in office buildings, and well, nearly everywhere. Even offices and apartments on first floor are up one flight (including my apartment). Only Ground levels are on the ground, I guess that makes sense.

I was 20 minutes late when I made it through the Therapist's door. She was obviously annoyed with me. (Did I tell you it is not acceptable to be late here, or early? When invited to a German's home, you must arrive on time, flowers or wine bottle in hand. It is customary, respectful, and expected.)

The visit was brief; she dismissed me precisely after 10 minutes. Although no one was waiting, my 30 minute session was over and it was time for me to go. I left with fond memories of waiting for doctor appointments back home.

Today I called my doctor for a physical therapist nearer my apartment. He is sending me to one just across the street this evening! I wish I had asked earlier.

From: Carol
To: LittleAli
Subject: **Illusive X-Rays**
Date: Fri, February 11, 2000

Today I had my first trip to a neurologist. He gave me tests to see if any nerve damage had been done. Thankfully, there is no permanent nerve damage, at least not yet. I didn't realize it, but I can't raise myself up on the ball of either foot, and can't stand on the ball of either foot. They definitely think the problem is in the spine and say I may need an operation. They are very thorough here and believe surgery should be the last option. I certainly agree.

When I left the apartment for the doctor this morning, I forgot to take my x-rays. As I was getting on the bus, I remembered them. After going back to the apartment and picking up the x-rays, I got on the next bus 10 minutes later.

When I left the doctor's office, I stopped in the hall to put on my coat, placed the x-rays on a nearby chair, and walked off without them again! Later I learned they had been picked up and taken into my doctor's office, instead of any of the other doctors' offices in that hall. Preparing to get off the bus at home, I suddenly couldn't find the x-rays! So I got off the bus, walked across the street, waited 15 minutes, and took the next bus back to the neurologist.

It was noon by the time I got the x-rays, so I stopped at a little café and had lunch: brats, potato salad, tomato, cucumber, and hot chocolate. I asked for coke, she probably thought I said cocoa. Now I know to ask for coca cola next time I prefer coke to hot chocolate. The hot chocolate was excellent, however.

By the way, it seems the x-rays show my lower back is curved inward, called Spondylolisthesis. It is putting pressure on the sciatic nerve and probably causing the pain and nerve problems. At least that's how I understand it.

I have another physical therapy session this evening, I think there is improvement. I really look forward to going back to work Monday. I'm scheduling all my appointments after work from then on, and hope health and healing happen fast!

From: Carol
To: LittleAli
Subject: **German Classes**
Date: Thursday, February 17, 2000

I am enjoying being back at work. With my schedule; classes only coming to the lab one or two times a week, teachers staying with students, and flexible scheduling for the 5th and 6th graders, it was probably easier for me to be absent than for any other teacher. I am grateful I didn't cause too much disruption for everyone, but I hope I don't need to be out again.

Lisa and I have been attending German classes two evenings so far. The school is a long distance away, we ride busses, and we're very tired after a day of work. It's really difficult for me, but very interesting. The 25 students represent 10 different countries, including Russia, Finland, Turkey, Poland, Georgia, Northern Africa, Czech Republic, and the two of us from the United States. The teacher speaks only German. There's so much I don't know; if I ask a question it needs to be in German, so I don't ask questions. The book and workbook are all in German, so I don't know how that will help. There is a cassette tape too, but it's all in German, so how can I know what they are saying? You know, I may get something out of this class, I hope, but it may not be much. I have to go alone tomorrow night. Lisa says she will be too tired! We are scheduled three nights a week until June. I feel failure coming on.

This is one night I need to hear the Street Musicians. They are usually everywhere, on the sidewalks, at shopping areas, in the train stations, and even in the underground tunnels. When they lift my spirits and put a spring in my step, I give them money. I could use a spring in my step tonight.

Guess what! The postman knows me! Last evening when I rushed home after work to quickly change clothes for physical therapy, the postman was waiting at the door of my apartment building with a package. He had seen me coming, said "Coffey?" I said "Yes" and he handed me my package. I said "Danke schön!" Maybe my package chasing days are finally over.

From: Carol
To: LittleAli
Subject: **Stepping Lightly**
Date: Tue, February 22, 2000

Tonight I was able to walk normally, fast, and with ease. Why? Well, it might have been the Margarita I had for dinner. The doctor said there was no nerve damage; only the pain was holding me back. Maybe the Margarita relaxed my muscles and took away the pain too, briefly. Some people walk funny when they've been drinking; I walk funny unless I have a drink. Too bad there are limits to that theory.

We found a wonderful Mexican restaurant and they make good Margaritas and delicious Mexican food! I love trying new restaurants and exploring different parts of the city. I think we'll be going back to this place often.

And about all that salt around a Margarita, I love that salt and believe scientists will someday realize it's the secret to a long life. After all, salt is a preservative; it's keeping me young!

From: Carol
To: LittleAli
Subject: **Rigorous Routines**
Date: Saturday, March 11, 2000

I'm sorry I haven't written sooner, I don't have much news. The daily routine is getting in the way of the adventures! I guess that's understandable, occasionally.

We purchased a new server in the lab. It's taken many long hours and even last weekend getting everything changed over and clearing out the bugs. Thanks to Jason, the high school genius, it's all working now and much better than before. We also added a new printer, scanner, and digital camera.

I'm still traipsing to those German classes three nights a week, doing physical therapy three times a week, and going for heat and massage treatments. This is cutting into my social life. And the German classes are a lost cause—or rather, I 'm a lost cause. At the last session, I spent 20 minutes trying to find the page she was teaching from. Looking around at the others near me, every one of them was on a different page. Hmmm—I don't think I'm the only one who's lost!!! I have made my decision: I will not return!

With all the appointments, I've still been able to have occasional dinners with friends at our local Italian and Chinese Restaurants. We have two Italian restaurants, each a block away in different directions; both are quite good. They both bring bruschetta with fresh tomato and basil as soon as we arrive, like they bring tortilla chips at Mexican restaurants at home. The Chinese Restaurant is about two blocks away. My favorite part of their dining experience is the complimentary Plum Wine they bring before each meal. It's a very small amount of a very tasty, very sweet, aperitif. Like most restaurants in Berlin, the vegetables and fruits are unbelievably fresh and seating is both inside and outside.

I got new glasses from a German eye doctor. Since my Lasik eye surgery a year ago, my eye doctors haven't been able to correct my vision to 20-20. The Lasik left me with about 20-40, now it's at 20-50. My new glasses only bring me to 20-40 and actually I don't notice much difference. The difficulty comes when I need to read signs—in subways, train stations, airports, and peering through bus windows at street signs to figure out when to get off. Since I was way more than legally blind before the surgery and I just couldn't tolerate the contacts anymore, I still think of the Lasik procedure as a miracle. My friends can read the signs before me, so they take the lead when we're together; when alone I am probably slower but also more focused and I notice more. I am glad I don't need to drive a car in this or any foreign country; sharper vision might be a necessity.

Putting it off as long as possible and fearing a lack of communication, I finally went to a dentist here for a cleaning and check-up. Thankfully this dentist spoke good English and was very gentle. Remember how I've been opposed to having metal fillings in my teeth although my dentist at home continued to assure me the metal fillings were safe and healthy? Now I have a whole country on my side! My German dentist told me metal fillings are no longer permitted in Germany (and Sweden, according to her). She did fill one of my teeth and I was so relieved not to have to fight to get the white composite fillings. This just confirms my trust in the health care here.

Last week several of us went downtown to the Neues Berliner Kabarett to see Americans speak! It was Garrison Keiler and his *Prairie Home Companion* public radio broadcast live here in Berlin! For one thing, it was just a very special treat to hear our language in a live performance, something we obviously take for granted at home. The whole performance was wonderful, very funny and exciting, with excellent performers. Never in a million years would I have expected to be in the audience of that show here in Berlin!

Next weekend, Lisa and I have been invited to the country home of a couple we teach with. I am so excited to get out of town, breath fresh country air, and relax with friends. They trekked in Nepal several years ago and promise us a slideshow of their adventures. Often, I think of Nepal and wish I could go back. There's something about that place that so deeply touched my heart. With my physical limitations, I may need to schedule that trip for my next life.

I am planning to visit Krysta in Baton Rouge for Spring Break in April. Then I'll go to Erin's Graduation in May and see both my daughters and my parents. This routine downtime is just a lull before all the action starts again.

I'm even making plans for a trip to Norway this summer. The German tours are in German, so I'm looking into British tours. Norway is such a huge country with so much variety; it's hard to decide which parts to leave out.

We have parent conferences Monday. Classes are dismissed at noon; parent conferences are scheduled until 8 pm. Although it will be a long day, I look forward to talking with the parents about their children. The parents here are so supportive and involved, the students are so motivated and talented; it's a win-win position. Our high school was rated as the best Berlin high school last year by the local newspaper, *Der Tagesspiegel*; it is an excellent school, and I think the parents are happy their students are able to attend here.

From: Carol
To: LittleAli
Subject: **German Country Home**
Date: Tuesday, March 21, 2000

Our weekend in the country was relaxing and beautiful. The house is elegant, furnished in antique German; it could have been pictured in a decorating magazine. Lisa and I were graciously pampered and entertained; I'm just not used to being treated so well. They are wonderful hosts, gourmet cooks, and everything was meticulously planned and fun. I especially enjoyed seeing slides of their trip to Nepal; I do miss that place.

Our activity Saturday afternoon was going to Yard Sales, searching for antique treasures for their home. This rich experience was far from my yard sale excursions at home; this was more about traipsing through history in the East German countryside.

Sunday afternoon I walked alone along the river for about three miles. The weather was very sunny and a little cool and breezy. It felt especially intoxicating, since I haven't been out in nature since the Switzerland trip. After not being able to walk much, this felt very exhilarating and freeing! I don't remember ever feeling so peaceful. And sleep was the deepest ever; such silence, only birds and a flowing river to break the spell.

Their historic country home is in a very small, very old East German village. Although North-West of here, it is part of old East Germany. I hadn't realized until I arrived in August, Berlin was a walled city fully surrounded by East Germany, but was politically considered West Germany. So as we travel around the city, we alternately go in and out of old East and West all the time.

Our friends are Americans who have taught here about 20 years. They bought the house in 1988, a year before the wall went down. It was Communist country then. I'm not sure how they could do that since they were living in Berlin at the time. They have done extensive renovation and are planning much more. They also do gardening and had fresh spinach, lettuce, and mint. Just being out in the country was such a treat! We were treated like royalty; I feel very spoiled and honored to have been invited.

Speaking of being spoiled, I had a German teacher telling me again today how happy she is with what I'm doing and what her students are doing in my lab, and how happy she is with what she's learning from me. I am not used to being complimented. The students get so excited with what they're able to do with their computer projects; I love it! They are also learning keyboarding with proper finger placement. The challenge comes with using two keyboards interchangeably; English and German. They have to be able to change to the one they need for any or all keys at any time. Since the keyboard is American, I've added the German differences with permanent marker on the appropriate keys. It helps immensely (for me, too!).

From: Carol
To: LittleAli
Subject: **Lost Day!**
Date: Saturday, April 15, 2000

Yesterday I spent the day getting lost! What a weird day! I just wanted to go to an S-Bahn stop about a half hour away and look at a poster for a Nepal slide show. I thought that would be simple! I should have realized I was off to a bad start when I walked out of my apartment and saw that I had just missed the bus and would have to wait 20 minutes.

When I got to the S-Bahn, the information said the slide show was tonight, in German. Since I'm flying to the United States tomorrow, I'll miss the slide show.

The subway station was Wannsee, on a beautiful lake that I love to visit. I spent some time walking along the lake and enjoying the boats, then waited at the bus stop to go home. Strangely, an unscheduled bus was in the place of my bus just before mine should be there. Looking closely, I saw my bus behind it and walked toward it. The door was shut, it was two minutes before scheduled arrival, and it pulled away! I was at the door; I guess he didn't see me. I had 20 more minutes to wait for the next bus.

I walked around and got back 10 minutes early. Five minutes before scheduled arrival, the 118 bus pulled up. I knew it goes close my apartment, so I decided to get on it. It took off but when it didn't turn at the next street, I realized I was going the wrong direction, way out of Berlin. I didn't even have the proper pass for it, but I decided to just go along for the ride. I could have gotten off at any stop, crossed the street, and hopped on another bus back to Wannsee, but I thought, ok, I'll be adventurous. I rode about 45 minutes to the end of the line. I was in Pottsdam. I saw a huge beautiful shopping center and remembered Lisa had told me she takes the S-Bahn there and loves it. Thinking I could get the S-Bahn from there back to Wannsee, I checked the place out. It was much like our malls and had some interesting shops.

Not seeing an S-Bahn, I asked several people. They told me to cross the highway, catch the 696 bus to the Bahnhoff. Funny, I didn't remember Lisa saying she had to take a bus from the S-Bahn, but I followed their directions and crossed the highway on the overpass (a 15 minute walk) to the bus stop and checked the schedule. Just then, the 696 bus pulled up, I turned to get on, and guess what? It pulled away!!! I must be invisible!!! I was right at the door and he just didn't see me.

Checking the schedule, it showed a 20 minute wait. Being a little impatient and a little disillusioned with this adventure by then, I decided to get back on the 118 bus, which was coming in 15 minutes, and ride the 45 minutes into Wannsee. Another woman joined me and then two junior high school boys came and waited with us. On schedule, the 118 bus drove right past us, didn't stop, and just ignored us! The boys were pretty mad and left.

I continued to wait for the 696 right at the curb, it did stop, and I got on! I tried to pay for a ticket and the driver waved his arms and said something emphatic; I thought it must be a free day for me! Then I asked, "S-Bahn seiben (seven)? He said "Bahnhof, ya." and waved me in. After five stops, he announced, "Bahnhof." and I got off.

I was totally in the middle of nowhere! Seeing only a couple of houses and some buildings, I started wandering around. At a distance, I noticed a tiny restaurant named Bahnhof something so I walked that way, but saw nothing else. Then a real person appeared. I must have looked lost because he said "Bahnhof?" and I said "ja." He pointed so I said "dankeshern" and started walking that way on a little path between buildings. Then he said "Berlin?" and I said "ja" and he pointed a different direction. So I thanked him again and walked to railroad tracks, crossed over, and saw a tiny sign, "Berlin". Seeing a schedule, I learned I was at the Regional train stopping place instead of at the S-Bahn. Now I know Bahnhof means the Regional train which takes us outside city limits; not the city transient S-Bahn!!! Big difference!!!

According to the schedule, the train would come in 45 minutes. I walked by a man who was also going to Berlin. We couldn't speak each other's languages, but I let him know I was going to check the bus (pronounced boose) schedules first—so I walked to three bus stops, but the 118 I wanted was not there, so I went back to the train stop. With 15 minutes to go, he showed me his ticket. I didn't have one. I thought on a train you could just get on, a conductor comes around and sells you a ticket if you don't have one. Well, it seems that was not going to work this time, so he took me across the tracks to a machine (never done that before!) and showed me how to check the train number (5656) I needed (I would never have had a clue on that one!) and punch in the numbers to see the price (equivalent to $1.80). Luckily I had the right change and got the ticket. He showed me how to get it stamped, as it is only good for two hours. He was really helpful. I showed him the map and how I wanted the S-Bahn; we were far from there. He made sure I got off the train at my stop. Thank goodness he was there, otherwise, I would have had a free ride on the train because no one came to check, but it's good I learn. If they check and you don't have a pass, they charge you a lot.

Finally, getting off at the Wannsee terminal, I took the 211 bus home--four hours later than planned!

This was a learning experience; hopefully it will help me in other situations. Luckily I had no plans for the day, but getting lost would not have been my choice. And I never was really upset. I was so calm and just relaxed and went with the flow. It wasn't a bad day, really. I just wonder why it happened like that. For awhile, I thought maybe the Universe was sending me to do something, see something, understand something, who knows? Well, maybe I was supposed to connect with that wonderful man who helped me, but we couldn't speak the same language. I think that's important. So if God is sending me a man, he'd better be able to speak my language because I don't seem to have the intellectual capacity to speak another language.

Now it's time to pack! I'm flying to Louisiana tomorrow morning to visit Krysta. I'm so excited to see her, and it will be interesting to understand conversations all around me and be able to speak and be understood!

Oh, I learned the deodorant I've been buying here is not an antiperspirant, only a deodorant. Antiperspirants are not sold here; they must think it's unhealthy. The containers look the same, I buy the same brand here as at home, but now I notice they don't say "antiperspirant." Since I'm going to the United States, land of antiperspirants, German friends have asked me to bring back a supply of that illicit product.

From: Carol
To: LittleAli
Subject: **Visiting Krysta**
Date: Monday, May 1, 2000

I had a great visit with Krysta for nearly two weeks and arrived back in Berlin Saturday. She showed me all around, we tried Zydeco dancing, took a boat trip on the Bayou, ate crab legs, shrimp and jambalaya, and went to her church on Sunday. She sings in the choir, so she dragged me into the practice room and somehow I ended up singing with the choir for the service. She works with the youth and is a busy girl, in church and at work too. Her home is beautiful, with big trees and a beautiful courtyard.

We had such fun together. I don't think she even got tired of me, and she said I could come back anytime for any length of time and that I could even live with her if I wanted. What a contrast from the teenage years! She's become such a sweet, wonderful, young woman.

When I arrived in Berlin, I was so surprised to see everything in bloom! What a beautiful city! My favorite is the Kastania trees. They are a European Chestnut, amazing all year long, beautifully shaped and so huge; I don't think

I've ever seen such big deciduous trees! I certainly know what Wordsworth meant by "Under the Spreading Chestnut Tree!" In the fall, Gretel proudly showed me the Kastania tree next to our school. It had ominous thorny chestnuts all over it and she warned me they could cause damage when they fell, even breaking windshields on cars parked beneath. Now they have taken on a whole new appearance! White and pink blooms are all over those huge trees! The blooms are about seven inches high, shaped like a cone with the small part at the top, made up of small delicate blossoms about half an inch each. It's hard to tell exactly because the trees are so high, even the lowest branches are up there pretty far, so I can't seen all the detail in the flowers. I just know these elegant giant trees are all over the city and take my breath away every time I see one. I believe the blooming Kastania trees are my favorite part of Berlin, and they were such a surprise, I was not warned of their beauty!

Today is another holiday, German Labor Day. Nothing is open, not even schools, so I am resting and putting things away. I am going to a party at 2 pm. It will be good to hear about everyone's holidays.

From: Carol
To: LittleAli
Subject: **Werder Festival**
Date: Monday, May 8, 2000

Lisa and I took a two hour boat trip Saturday from Wannsee, down the River Havel to Werder on the Havel. When we got off the boat, their famous Blossoming Festival was in full swing! What fun, lots of music, arts and crafts, and very happy people. The hit of the party was their locally made fruit wines sold in easy to open, convenient to carry, just the right size plastic bottles. Fruits grown in the area are cherries, apples, strawberries, raspberries, gooseberries, currants, blackberries, apricots, peaches, pears, and plums. I tried a couple of different flavors and caught the festive spirit!

And almost ended up with a boyfriend! A good looking young Pakistani man flirted, asked for my phone number, and asked me out. He was quite persuasive; I think he learned the English language from romance novels. When I told him I was way too old for him, he proudly confided that he was 29 and had a college degree. I didn't acknowledge I lacked only one year of being double his age, I just acted surprised he was that old and turned him down. He did make me laugh and I will admit, boosted my ego, and made my day. I'll never know his real motives; just money, maybe sex, maybe even a Green Card to get into America! I reminded myself, a woman just can't be too careful!

I'm flying to Erin's Graduation Wednesday! I am so excited!

From: Carol
To: LittleAli
Subject: **Erin's Graduation**
Date: Tuesday, May 16, 2000

Erin's graduation from Webster University in St. Louis was wonderful. Her degree is a BFA in Stage Management, she graduated *cum laude* and was one of ten students pictured on the Commence Program cover. Was I proud? You bet I was!!!

It was a quick five day trip packed with non-stop special moments. Erin and her roommate were such good hostesses. We all had a good time, the activities were easy to get to and well organized; the campus was beautiful; even the weather cooperated.

I had the honor of staying with Erin and her roommate in their apartment. The others stayed in a motel. Krysta was with her dad and his mom from Colorado, my parents drove from West Virginia, and Erin's Aunt Sally came from Minnesota. With my parents nearly 80, I was quite worried about them driving so far, but thankfully they had a safe trip.

Erin will be Stage Manager at Creede Repertory Theater this summer in the mountains of Colorado. She has worked there in recent summers; it's a fantastic experience in a magical setting, and a lot of fun too.

From: Carol
To: LittleAli
Subject: **Prague by Train**
Date: Monday, May 29, 2000

What a Memorial Day Weekend! No hotdogs, potato salad, picnics, or fire works—but it was fantastic! Eleven of us left Friday after work, backpacks on our backs, and traveled by train into The Czech Republic to the romantic pink city of Prague. If I could paint, that is where I would go to paint. Everyone was doing it, the whole city is just so artistic; it truly inspires!

Gretel, my German friend and our German librarian, shared a room with me. Laura was our volunteer leader and led us on foot and subway to a castle, cathedral, graveyard,

Marionette Theater, sidewalk artist displays, elegant restaurants, and streets lined with awe-inspiring architecture dating back to the 1300's.

We toured the Gothic castle and St. Vitus' Cathedral founded by Good King Wenceslas. Art Nouveau accents adorn many buildings; my eyes were on the architecture as I tried to keep up along uneven cobblestone streets.

After an elegant dinner in a magnificent restaurant with very filling meats and potatoes, Laura took us to see Mozart's opera, Don Giovanni, done exclusively by stylish life-sized marionettes. What a treat! Prague is Mozart's hometown and Don Giovanni was first performed there in 1787.

The Jewish Cemetery was crowded! Jewish people were only given a small area to bury their dead. Consequently, some bodies are buried upright to save space, others are stacked horizontally. Grave stones are haphazardly standing on nearly every square inch of sacred ground. Although this was a grim reminder of the past, I was relieved to learn this city was spared; no bombs fell in this precious place.

In the Jewish Synagogue, I was amazed and disturbed to learn that the women could only watch the service from the small enclosed balcony, peering through rectangular holes about 1 ft by 2 ft. I assume that was during and before the war and hope that's not still occurring anywhere today.

I took some time away from my friends, wandered the streets, gazed at the famous town clock, and just let the romance of the city wash over me. I strolled across the St. Charles Bridge, stepping lightly to the music of minstrels, opera singers, and Bavarian dancers. Exclusively a walking bridge, it is lined with artists, crafters, and musicians. I bought a beautiful necklace and earring set made of leather which looks like wood in a subtle shape of an angel. I also bought some very small paintings, and a realistic architectural scene sculpted in leather. The St. Charles Bridge is my favorite part of Prague. The Elbe River is very wide and the view from the bridge is exquisite.

Color-coded maps made the subway system easy to navigate. Everything went smoothly except when we were approached by a very angry man yelling something we couldn't understand. When we didn't respond, he yelled louder! Others came over and showed him their ticket. That seemed to calm him down, so we did the same. I guess it's an honor system similar to Germany's, everyone buys a ticket and it's seldom checked. But in Prague, they check with more noise than the calm, orderly, authoritative Germans.

I had three college guys spending the night here last night; Laura's son and two friends camped out on my couch, foldout foam chair, and tiny twin bed. They went with us to Prague and were such fun to be with.

From: Carol
To: LittleAli
Subject: **German Alps**
Date: Tuesday, June 6, 2000

I just got back from the German Alps! The occasion as the German Holiday called Himelfarht (Ascension Day); we had Thursday and Friday free. I went to the Bavarian section of Germany between Munich and the Austrian border. I stayed in the little village of Grainau right at the base of the Zugspitze, the highest mountain in Germany. It's just four miles from Garmish, where your daughter and family are going to live for awhile. It is really beautiful. Traveling solo from Berlin by high speed train, I changed to a very small train in Munich and really enjoyed the scenic countryside from that point on. I have been missing the mountains; they are my drug of choice!

I wore my real Colorado Hiking Boots most of the time and it felt so good to be hiking again! The high point was my excursion to the top of the Zugspitze, it's only 10,000 ft or so but the top is a long way to the bottom, so it looks just as high as the Swiss Alps. Austria and Germany share the mountain, so I was able to cross over in to Austria at the top. So now I have been in Austria!

When I went up the mountains, I rode a little old train which took us inside the mountain for nine miles. Then I rode a cable car to the top where unbelievable scenery in all directions competed with a restaurant and gift and outdoor clothing shops. I guess civilizing mountains is a European thing, not exclusively Swiss. I could see the Italian, Swiss, Austrian, and German Alps from up there; what a view! I decided to go all the way down by cable car, I could see so much more than I could from the train inside the mountain. I am always energized by high altitude, so I was full of energy when I got back, so I walked four miles around a beautiful lake, called Eibsee; then stopped at a café on the mountain for dinner. I took a bus back to my hotel.

There are so many trails; I spent the next day hiking. I also went back to the lake and the café on the mountainside. The weather was perfect, the sky was blue, like in Colorado, and we had sunshine all day! People here are much more relaxed, smiling, and friendly than strangers in Berlin. I am learning that is the Bavarian style. Their language is a little different too, and they greet you with "Grüss Gott" instead of "Guten Tag or Morgen", so I greeted them their way. The houses are chalet style like Switzerland, it is a farming area. I love it here! Your daughter is going to love it here; it will be wonderful for your grandchildren.

Meanwhile, work goes on, with meetings and teaching, it's all good. We've had several Hitzefrei days last week, getting out at 1 pm because it's 77 degrees by 11am. I love that tradition!

I have a new doctor; she's an osteopath from America. After marrying a German, she got a medical degree here and has been a practicing German physician for about 15 years. I really like her and I love that she speaks English so well! To begin our sessions, she checks my tongue and takes my pulse using the Aryuvadeic method (taught by Deepak Chopra) which checks functions of the liver and some other parts. I wonder if this is German, or just Aryuvadeic from India. Other than sending me to physical therapists and for massage and heat treatments, she is giving me Acupuncture sessions two or three times a week. That does seem to be helping. All doctors here are trained in Acupuncture. The first time she gave me an Acupuncture treatment, I had been sitting in her waiting room for an hour and a half; it was after 6 pm, and I was the last person waiting. We had the regular office visit; then I was put on a heat/vibration bed to relax my muscles for 20 minutes. The Acupuncture followed that, I was placed in a room by myself with the door closed. After about 20 minutes when the treatment was supposed to be completed, I didn't hear any noises outside my room. I began to fear the doctor and staff had gone home and I was left there for the night with needles in my back. By the time the nurse came in 15 minutes later to release me, I was ready to get out of there!

The thing I love most about trips to the doctor is the Kastania trees in the area. There is one especially impressive tree alongside a restaurant I usually stop at for dinner. The weather is usually good, most places do not have air conditioning, and most everyone dines outside this time of year. I love sitting outside and gazing up into that magnificent tree, especially when it was in bloom.

We have another 3-day weekend coming up. Next Monday is Pentecost. I plan to do something different: nothing! I'm just glad to have that extra day.

From: Carol
To: LittleAli
Subject: **Duct Tape Survival**
Date: Wednesday, June 7, 2000

I'm still finding things I can't find here! Can you believe I can't find Duct Tape? Somehow I thought it would be a universal necessity. The roll I brought is nearly gone and I just don't want to be without that survival tool. From the time I learned its life-saving uses in Colorado Mountain Club's *Mountaineering First Aid* class, my duct tape goes with me everywhere and really came in handy on my trip to Nepal last May. When we were in a van driving the narrow curvy road from the jungle of Chitwan National Park to the beautiful city of Pokhara near the Annapurna Mountains, the engine stopped working. Our guide said there was a leak in something or other. I suggested Duct Tape. Although the driver said it wouldn't work, our much wiser guide said it might. They used my tape; it totally worked! Frankly, they didn't even get the van fixed when they got to

Pokhara, the duct tapped repair got us into Kathmandu on schedule a few days later.

I promised my daughters an all-expense paid trip to Germany with a personal tour guide to show them the sights. Erin doesn't know when she can come, but Krysta took me up on it and is coming Saturday for nine days. I am so excited to see her and show her my new world! We will be going to the German Alps I just visited. It's so beautiful; I know she'll love it! And guess what? She's bringing Duct Tape!

From: Carol
To: LittleAli
Subject: **Krysta comes to Germany**
Date: Monday, July 17, 2000

Krysta arrived last Friday; we had a great time! I'm so happy she was here and was so sad to see her leave; like a part of me left on that plane. We walked the streets near my apartment, went around the clothing optional Schlachtensee Lake near here, ate in my favorite Berlin restaurants, rode a little ferry boat to Pfaueninsel (Peacock Island) Castle, and toured several tourist spots. She was becoming familiar with the busses and subway systems and decided to master the German language during this visit!

We spent five glorious days in the German Alps, so she is also quite familiar with the train systems now. Although the weather was cold and rainy and cloudy, we had a wonderful experience! I took her everywhere I went when I was there and more. We stayed in Uber Grainau, which is a little closer the base of the Zugspitze than Grainau. Our cable car ride to the Zugspitze top took us through the clouds and above them. Being Colorado Girls, we found the air up there exhilarating and Krysta was thrilled with the fresh snow; something she doesn't see much in Louisiana.

With raincoats and umbrellas, we walked around Eibsee Lake and went to the tourist spots and cafes but they were all closed. Signs on the doors said something about the weather being so bad they had decided to take the day off! That might not have been normal July weather for them. It was a contrast to the crowds and 70 degree sunny days I spent there in May and June. Again, being from Colorado, we enjoyed the cold summer weather and especially enjoyed the lack of crowds. On a rainy evening, we visited an ancient church and cemetery in town. Here and in Switzerland, the plots are immaculate, with fresh flowers, elaborate headstones, and beautiful landscaping.

Our train trip to Mittenwald was amazing. It's a small historic Bavarian ski town next to the Austrian border nestled at the base of Karwendel Spitze, Germany's second highest mountain. Colorful flowers grow everywhere, buildings are painted with murals depicting life on earth and in heaven, and music of the famous Mittenwald violins fill the air. It is the perfect setting for a fairytale, only Prince Charming was missing.

On our return trip from Grainau, we changed trains in Munich; then stopped for a couple of hours in Nuremburg. Although the Christmas decorations and festivities were gone, it is still a beautiful old medieval city this time of year. We stashed our bags in a train station locker, had lunch in a 14th century old stone restaurant built out over the river, visited the cathedrals, and toured the city. During my Christmas trip, we tried to eat at that restaurant but it was full and no reservations were available the entire weekend.

Back in Berlin, we took a day trip by train to Wittenberg. I had been there by car with Gretel, now I know how to get there by train. I think Krysta enjoyed seeing where Martin Luther nailed his 95 theses to the church door in 1517, bringing about the Protestant Reformation.

Krysta left yesterday and I went for an MRI today. Since I have claustrophobia, my doctor prescribed valium and Lisa went with me. I hardly felt the valium, but I didn't have any problems being in that cylinder. Lisa and I went shopping and out to lunch afterwards, exploring this unfamiliar part of Berlin. The MRI showed I had a slipped, ruptured, herniated disc in the spot where my spine is out of alignment; the disc is sticking out quite far. I guess that's what's pressing on that Sciatic nerve. Well, it gives my doctors more information; hopefully they can make me all well.

It's really wonderful you're going with your daughter to the Dolomites in Italy and to Austria. I'm excited to hear about your trip.

From: Carol
To: LittleAli
Subject: **Sweden by Ferry**
Date: Tuesday, July 25, 2000

I just got back from a solo trip to Sweden. I took an 11 pm train and paid for a sleeping berth. The train was ancient and rickety; the berth was a shelf on the wall!!! My assigned compartment had six shelves, three on each side, to sleep six people! The aisle between was just wide enough for me to navigate, my shelf was in the middle. A man slept above me; a child slept below. With no place for my luggage, I slept with it under my feet. With no air conditioning or air circulation and the door closed, we opened the window. The Swedish mother of two children closed the window; she didn't want a draft on her children. Frankly, it was miserable. With claustrophobia and a need for fresh air, I took a few deep breaths, practiced my relaxation techniques, and at midnight, went to sleep! I'm shedding my old phobias; and fears and learning acceptance and patience.

When I awoke at 5am, the others were gone. People were coming in and out of the train. I couldn't figure that out. It felt like we were moving, but not the normal way. We were definitely in motion but it was quieter, no train on the tracks sound. I figured if others could get off the train, I'd do that too. Wow! Our train was in the bottom of a humongous boat! Cars were parked down there too. I walked up the steps and found I was on a ferry crossing the Baltic Sea! I had wondered how we'd be crossing the Baltic; if there was a tunnel like from England to France, or if there was a big bridge. Who knew a train could float on water, even in a big boat?

It turned out we had been on the water four hours. I could have slept on the upper deck in the open air in a lounge chair! That would have been heavenly, all the open space and fresh air I could imagine! Oh well, I am wiser now and was excited to sit on the top deck during the return daytime trip. After we arrived in Copenhagen, I took a lovely train trip through southern Sweden, enjoying the rolling hills and quaint pastoral scenes.

Sweden was very cold and rainy; or at best, gray and cloudy. Watching the news I learned Northern Sweden was being flooded and that flood waters would reach my area just after I left. Good timing! The village of Ronneby had beautiful flowers and gardens, lots of scenic hiking trails, and a quiet river with gentle walking paths along its banks. The one mile walk from my luxurious hotel and spa to the village was very pleasant. It was a perfect opportunity to rest, read, and walk in the country. The green rolling hills reminded me of West Virginia. The houses are small and very clean and neat, with lots of beautiful flowers and well manicured lawns. I couldn't speak Swedish, but most people knew some English. I could read some signs; there seems to be a German influence in the language, although the Swedish words are much shorter than German.

On the return trip, I rode a train across the country to Copenhagen, and then got on another train for the ride across the Baltic. Since it was daytime, I could see where I was and what was going on. That ferry boat was more like a Cruise Ship. I got to watch them put the train on the third floor (deck); that's ground level. There were only two train cars this time, no engine. I assumed there'd be an engine waiting on the other side.

We were free to go in and out of the train, so we all went up into the ship. The restaurant, bar, casino, and shops were on the 7th level; the 8th and 9th levels were outdoor decks. The weather was cold and foggy; I could hardly see the water. I enjoyed wandering around; then sat down with a glass of wine in an oversized padded chair in the bar, right by the window, and read a captivating book most of the afternoon. Later, I enjoyed a delicious dinner in the restaurant. When we got to the German island of Rugen where I had spent Thanksgiving, the magnificent White Cliffs were a welcome sight as the sun came out to make them glisten like diamonds.

The trip was very pleasant and restful, the pastoral countryside was beautiful, but I didn't feel I really learned much about Sweden on this trip.

Norway will be my next stop. I'll be doing a two week British tour through mountains and fjords by bus and ferry at the end of this week. On my first overseas trip at the age of 55, my roommate predicted I was catching the "Travel Bug" and that trip would be the beginning of many travel adventures for me. I disagreed, saying that Swiss trip was my once-in-a-lifetime outside the country travel; I would never be able to afford to travel again. I am so glad she was right and I was wrong!

From: Carol
To: LittleAli
Subject: **British Tour of Norway**
Date: Sunday, Aug 20, 2000

Deep blue fjords, abundant waterfalls, lush green vegetation, expansive glistening glaciers, majestic mountains, illusive mischievous trolls hiding behind rocks and trees, lakes reflecting mirror images of breathtaking scenery, 360 degree breathtaking panoramas, pastoral landscapes, children playing on vertical hillside yards safely tethered above dangerous fjords, grass growing on rooftops, bountiful wilderness; Norway's wild beauty ranks among the best on this earth!

For the past two weeks, I've been touring Norway with Anna, a good friend from my college days. During our early careers, we shared an apartment in the Washington, DC area. Recently retired from her government position in DC and living in West Virginia now, she flew to London and joined me on a British tour of Norway. It was such fun to be with her on this adventure. We were the only non-Brits on the coach (that's what they call busses.) Everyone was so sweet, kind, interesting, and fun to be with. When the tour ended, we exchanged hugs, addresses, and promises to keep in touch.

Our tour started in Oslo, took us through the historic Telemark region where we rode a boat down the Telemark Canal through locks from Ulefoss to Lunde. When that got too slow, we walked alongside the canal to stretch our legs and get our exercise for the day. Back on the bus, we were taken through the Rjukan Gorge for a tour of the historic and impressive Vemark Power Station. I was fascinated to learn how Hitler tried to overtake this lake of heavy water, and how the strong and heroic Norwegians skied over the mountains in winter to save their Power Plant and to keep Hitler's forces from continuing on to overtake Britain.

After climbing out of the Gorge we drove through wild snowy mountains of the Hardangervidda and on to the fjords with mountains rising 6000 ft above. Our coach boarded the lower deck of the ferry while we explored the upper decks for our cruise the length of Sørfjord, passing the magnificent Folgefonn Glacier, with waterfalls and spectacular scenes with every turn.

On the other end of the fjord, we boarded our coach and traveled over extremely narrow zigzag hairpin-curved paved mountain roads, inching to pass the cars which were inching safely past us. From there we were above timberline surrounded by jagged peaks, seeing panoramic vistas of Norway from the top. Melting snowfields on mountain peaks displayed inkblot-like reflections in mountain lakes; I snapped pictures from the moving bus.

While stopped in the picturesque village of Ulvik, we were privileged to see a wedding procession. Participants were dressed in traditional costumes of their village (costumes differ with geographic area). I discretely followed at a distance, taking pictures and enjoying this glimpse of local customs.

Medieval Stave Churches from Viking days were fascinating, made completely of wood outside and in, with detailed wood carvings of their Pagan deities. We visited the Heddal Stave Church near Vradal and traveled through the Vik mountains to the Hoppestad Stave Church.

My favorite trip was riding the ferry on the Sognfjord from Vangsnes to Balestrand, then on the most spectacular Fjærlandsfjord. We visited the Glacier Centre at Fjærland. I was so thrilled by the wide screen cinema of glaciers and wild mountains, I got permission to view it a second time. After that, we walked out on Boyum glacier, but only the edge. We didn't get close to the vast wilderness of ice pictured on the screens. I began to realize there's so much more of Norway that I will never see, but it's fascinating to know about it and that some humans do venture out there.

While staying three nights in Loen, we were able to take a boat trip on Lake Loen to the Kjenndal Glacier and cruise on the unbelievably beautiful Geirangerfjord past more waterfalls than I've ever seen in one area. From there our ride to the top of Mount Dalsnibba was one of the most beautiful sights of the trip. After leaving Loen and traveling along calm Lake Jolster, we were treated to perfect reflections of the surrounding hills. After our last ferry ride, Lavik/Opdal, we stayed in Bergen. Located on the sea, this large city has the feel of a small fishing village, with fish markets and colorful old wooden buildings along the bay.

The coach, ferries, and boats were very comfortable. The hotels were some of Norway's best with excellent accommodations, including breakfasts and dinners. Dinners were usually delicious buffets specializing in seafood, and always included my new favorite cheese; a brown dessert goat cheese called Gjetost which tasted like caramel. Very strong and sweet, I only partook of a very thin slice after each meal.

It was an expensive two weeks, but for the first time in my life I have money and needed to be guided and catered to on this trip. Now I want to go back to explore on my own. We only got about half way up that long narrow country; I want to get into the Arctic Circle on the next trip. This is a wonderland! And most everyone speaks English!

During our three night stay at Loen, Anna caught a cold. It was my fault. I wanted the window open and heat off; she was kind and didn't say a word. I know she was pretty miserable the rest of the trip and I felt very bad about it all.

Did you know our cardigans are called jumpers in England? Anna bought a beautiful Norwegian Cardigan sweater and wore it on the cooler days. People kept complimenting her on her jumper. At first we just wondered what they were talking about; finally it became evident it was her new sweater. We wondered what they would call our jumpers, but weren't sure how to ask.

After Norway, Anna joined me in Berlin for a few days. Her cold was finally over and we had a great time seeing the sights of Berlin and taking a train trip into old Eastern Germany to Wittenberg, my favorite tourist town, and to the historic city of Dresden the next day. It is pathetic that we bombed this beautiful city just after the war was over.

Thankfully, the city is being reconstructed to its old grandeur; it is an amazing place. We visited a castle, a palace, the magnificent Church Frauenkirche, and took a tour bus with English speaking ear phones around the Altstadt (old town) displaying government buildings, museums, and art galleries in 18th century Baroque architecture. On foot, we explored the galleries and shops which specialized in crystal and delicate China. Anna bought me a genuine China demitasse cup and saucer, almost too elegant and fragile to drink from. I will be adding it to my wonderful German Wall Shelving Unit. Wall Units are very common here and I'm enjoying filling mine with travel treasures and memories of special places.

The train trip was not perfect. Anna was hassled by the ticket taker because her ticket had been purchased from a travel agent and looked a little different. Luckily a couple of well-traveled students who spoke English and understood this was the right ticket, came to her rescue. With no air conditioning on that old train and 90 degree temperatures, we had our windows open. Everyone had their windows open except the woman behind us. She had the nerve to ask us to close our windows because she was feeling a draft!!! We did as she asked, but soon moved to another seat by an open window where we could feel a draft too.

I'm so glad you were able to do the Pikes Peak Ascent! Quoting you, "Not bad for a 70 year old broad!" Congratulations again and again!

From: Carol
To: LittleAli
Subject: **Back to School**
Date: Monday, September 4, 2000

I have even more compassion for Anna now since I got her cold after she left. It was one of the worst I've had; I almost couldn't teach the first day of school. I am really enjoying being back at work, the kids are so sweet and cute and the computers are working! Life is good!

I recently made reservations to go back to Kandersteg, Switzerland for Christmas. It may be my last opportunity for a Christmas in Switzerland; I wanted to make my reservations before Switzerland is full (as the Travel Agent told me last year.)

Can you believe it, we're on vacation again; it's German Labor Day! Gretel took me in her car to the little town of Luckau about two hours away. This year they had the flower festival for the area of Brandenburg, called the "Landesgartenschau". The festival moves to different cities each year. With colorful flower displays everywhere, it was a magical city in bloom. We were captivated by this quaint old East German village. Although the weather was cold and rainy, we took refuge in a warm café, drank a mug of glühwein, and were soon ready to tiptoe through the blossoms.

I got a kit from IKEA to make a bed! I'm beginning to realize most of my furniture came from IKEA. With many mistakes and more laughter, Lisa and I put it together Friday night. Sleeping on two almost twin-sized stacked mattresses on the floor grew tiresome! Germans don't use box springs, they just have slats and one mattress and a frame. Now I have a whole big wide bed made of the two nearly twin mattresses on slats and a frame. I bought a luxurious genuine 100% Goose Down-filled duvet (comforter) with about a foot of loft in height! This is a real splurge and I expect it to last for my lifetime!* I also splurged on a 400 thread count cotton duvet cover decorated with rosebuds. Although it is traditional to only have a duvet and a bottom sheet on a bed, I prefer to use a top sheet too. When I stay in European hotels, they change the duvet cover daily. I'm just going to change my top sheet weekly.

Please say hello to the *Wildflowers.* Your Aspen trip sounds like such fun, I do wish I could have been there for the hiking and camaraderie, I know you all had a wonderful weekend.

---

*Ten years later, I am still enjoying this luxurious duvet which is still in perfect condition.

From: Carol
To: LittleAli
Subject: **Witches and Home Brew**
Date: Tuesday, September 19, 2000

This weekend I went to the Harz Mountains north of here about three hours via regional train. The mountains are only 3000 ft high but are lovely rolling hills that remind me of West Virginia. We rode a very old very small steam powered train (Schmalspurbahnen) as it climbed switch-backs up the steep grade for a couple of hours to the top of Brocken, the highest mountain. This summit served as a Soviet high-tech listening post to spy on near-by American and British NATO forces. Civilized amenities such as restaurant and gift shop awaited our arrival. Witches abound there; their magic has been part of the folklore for centuries. According to local lore, witches gather for Walpurgisnacht, the April 30 (May Eve) celebration in these mountains. I enjoyed lunch; then bought a cute little old witch on skis for my Wall Unit Shelves.

The trip down the mountain was definitely different from the ascent. Shortly after departing, a man came down the aisle with a big basket of decorative miniature liquor bottles. They were filled with about three sips of some kind of strong home brew. I bought one; it was much stronger than wine. I think it's an acquired taste. They were a big hit and soon people were talking louder, laughing more, and the party began! This is the first time I've seen the usually reserved Germans be so rowdy. About an hour later, the train broke down. It struggled to hobble into a tiny village where we got off to wait for a local bus for the rest of our journey. That home brew made the long wait tolerable and soothed frayed nerves.

Erin has left her summer job in the Colorado mountains and has moved to Salt Lake City for a full time stage manager position in a theater there. She seems to be enjoying it so far. It's an exciting time for her and I'm so glad she's doing well.

Well, best wishes as you prepare for your European trip. I too am sorry we won't be able to connect on this trip. And about the money, you can't really put a price on precious experiences. It's so wonderful you have your health and strength to be able to hike in the Alps. Just celebrate that and enjoy every moment. When you think of what's important in life, and where the priorities are, I don't think saving money is very high on that list. In the big life review, I think we'll look back at good times, happiness, and friendships and I don't think we'll care at all that we saved some money. We can't take it with us. So enjoy the "play money". Hopefully your dollar will go farther here. Yesterday the exchange rate was 2.29 DM per dollar. It was 1.75 when I was hired, so I make less than I had estimated, but as long as I spend it here, it doesn't matter what the US exchange rate is. It's great for you right now.

From: Carol
To: LittleAli
Subject: **On Crutches!**
Date: Tuesday, October 3, 2000

Did you know German Crutches don't come up under your arm like the ones at home? You hold onto something like a bicycle handlebar and a brace rests against your lower arm about nine inches above. I am learning to use them now—because I tore the meniscus in my left knee! Running to catch a bus after work last week, my knee twisted and something in the back of the knee popped! I almost fell because I couldn't tolerate any weight on that knee. Luckily taxis wait near bus stops at S-Bahn stations, so a taxi was a few feet away. Suddenly getting on the bus was no longer a goal; I turned and struggled toward the taxi. I had to cross a small street; I've never crossed a street so slowly. It seemed the taxi driver could have pulled up for me, but I guess they have rules. He waited behind his line until I finally got to his door.

At my apartment, he helped me to the entrance. From there, I just sat down on the steps and scooted up to my door. Thankfully, Germans are very clean and our steps are mopped at least once a week. Inside, I used the back of a wooden chair from my dining room as my crutch.

Luckily I was able to get to an orthopedic surgeon the next day. That taxi driver came up the steps to get me at my request and later helped me to the office building entrance. From there, a very thoughtful man loaned me one of his crutches and I got up the steps and in to see the same doctor he was going to. With the help of an X-Ray and an Ultrasound, the doctor determined my meniscus was torn and gave me a magic injection and a pair of crutches. After 24 hours, I was able to put some weight on the leg and am getting along well with the crutches. I did try a knee brace—but German knee braces are very sturdy and heavy; so heavy it slid down my leg regardless of how tight I adjusted the Velcro. I should be walking on my own in about a week.

From: Carol
To: LittleAli
Subject: **Tromsø Trip**
Date: Sunday, Nov 5, 2000

Last night I got back from a glorious Fall Break trip to Tromsø, Norway. Located 217 miles into the Arctic Circle, Tromsø is in the middle of the Aurora Borealis (Northern Lights) zone, and is one of the best places in the world to view them. Although the culture, weather, and landscape of Northern Norway are quite different from Central and Southern Norway, the people are still friendly and many speak English, making it easier for me to get around on my own.

This time of year, sunlight is short (11am – 2 pm) but light just below the horizon gives a glow from about 10 am – 3 pm. On my departure Saturday morning, the sun was not visible although it was daylight. I kept trying to see the sun just below the horizon as we took flight, but it was not in sight. The sun stays low and in your eyes all day, but the light is amazingly bright and colorful. The long shadows, clear air and vivid light created a surreal magical appearance; lifting my spirits and boosting my energy.

While having supper Sunday night, I asked the receptionist where I could see the Northern Lights. She said to walk down the street and away from the city lights. As I was continuing my meal, her phone rang with news that the Lights were On! She told me I could see them now if I went outside. Only a couple of blocks away, I sat on an old stone wall and watched the Northern Lights dancing across the sky in white and green glowing patterns for about 20 minutes until they faded away. First I saw just a thin cloud; then I noticed a funnel moving around like a whip, seeming to touch the horizon with one end while its other end extended from a cloud. Soon a wider streak of light came from another direction, looking like a baby seal; then curved around like a swan. This display was my first encounter, and I was blessed to see the light displays three more nights on this trip; their appearance seems to be unpredictable and always a pleasant surprise.

I met a girl from Singapore who said she came just to see the Northern Lights. Since I had also come to see the Lights, it struck me how I may be more similar to someone across the world than to people near me; none of my friends were interested in this trip.

I love my plain little room with twin beds in the Ami Hotel, located on a hill overlooking the city center of charming colorful old wooden houses. The $65 per night is cheap for Norway; the room is very small and is up two flights of stairs. As in most of Europe, there is no lift (elevator). It is an end room with two windows for cross ventilation. My windows were open all night, bringing in the crisp freezing fresh air as I cuddled under two duvets (comforters) from both beds. Even after all that fresh air, the room still smelled of smoke, so I started sniffing and realized the curtains were the culprits. Removing the curtains, I placed them in a hall closet with the receptionist's permission. Later I lit a candle and never noticed the smoke smell again. Before I left, I re-hung the curtains.

As in most of Europe, smoking is acceptable nearly everywhere. I am adjusting. I have found I get a constant tickly cough from old smoke but fresh smoke just annoys me, makes my hair and clothes smoky, and gives me a light headache.

When I arrived Saturday night, the sky was clear with lots of bright stars. I looked out my windows for Northern Lights every time I woke throughout the night, but saw only twinkling stars and lights of the buildings and the harbor. A light snow covered the city Sunday morning, cars slid on the hilly streets; I walked carefully in my winter boots; cold temperatures kept the snow from melting.

Sunday was very quiet. Nothing opened until 1 pm, so I walked around the town, down to the harbor, and explored until I happened upon an open building, the Polar Museum located in an 1837 wharf house, depicting amazing views of Arctic hunting; Arctic expeditions; and the Sámi (Laplanders) people, nomads who follow the reindeer and live in teepees. So different from anything I've ever experienced, I was fascinated to learn all about this place. Later, other tourist attractions and restaurants opened and I had a busy afternoon touring a very old wooden Tromsø Cathedral and the inspiring modern Arctic Cathedral, looking much like the beautiful Air Force Academy Chapel at home.

Monday I walked to the small bus station and boarded a bus at 4 pm. I changed busses once and went on two ferries before boarding the Coastal Express (ship traveling the coast daily) at 9 pm to ride down the coast to Tromsø, arriving at midnight. The bus driver took my ticket, then handed it over to the next bus driver and told him where I would be getting off or changing busses. It's a very personal method, but I think it would be difficult if there were many passengers. Maybe it was just because I was a foreigner.

From the bus windows, I was able to see some Northern Lights by putting my coat over my head to block out the bus lights. Snowy mountains were visible throughout the journey, with occasional glimpses of flickering lights from farms and homes scattered along the way.

Boarding the Coastal Express, I was surprised it was so large, with a restaurant, gift shops, a bar, a TV room, and sleeping rooms. I was the only person to brave the slick decks and nearly unbearable cold out there; I cherished the peace, solitude, and invigorating atmosphere. Standing on the frigid icy deck of the Coastal Express, gazing up at the mesmerizing Northern Lights dancing all over the sky for three hours as we cruised past islands of snow-covered mountains in the Norwegian Sea, I knew this was where I most wanted to be in the whole world at that moment. The Northern Lights were performing during my entire trip, how fortunate is that?

Tuesday I realized it was Halloween in the U.S.; a reminder that I was in another part of the world. At 12:45 pm I boarded another public bus for Lyngseidet to travel through the Lyngs Alps by land and return by ferry. When we arrived in Lyngseidet, a village of 800 located on a two mile wide isthmus, I had an hour to wait in the grocery store and gift shop, and gaze at a huge plastic Santa with a Troll face. Named Gollis, it was voted Norway's ugliest tourist attraction. While there I was intrigued to read lodging was available in homes of residents. After an hour, I was the only person to board the next bus. As soon as got on the bus, the driver told me the ferry wasn't running due to the snow, wind, and poor visibility. I decided to go back the way I came and he graciously showed me the schedule with a two hour wait in a café in Nordkjosbotn. I didn't mind, I was having an adventure with no timeline and no special expectations, so off we went. In ten minutes, we arrived in Nordkjosbotn, and after a short discussion with another bus driver, my sweet driver said I could take that unscheduled bus back to Tromsø; it was leaving in five minutes. As usual the driver gave my ticket to the next bus driver and told him where to take me; I love being spoiled with such personal attention.

My bus arrived in Tromsø at 6 pm. Since it had been dark for hours, it felt like midnight! Although I hadn't eaten since breakfast, I didn't feel hungry. At 8 pm, I went down for a delicious Supper of vegetable soup, dry crackers, and my favorite Gjetost cheese at my hotel. A gorgeous man I had noticed at breakfast sat across from me. Probably in his late 20's, he had dark hair, was very muscular, clean cut, and extremely handsome. We tried to talk but our only common language was German and he couldn't speak or understand it any better than I could. He did communicate that he was a Russian diver here on business for two nights. He gave me his room number and invited me to visit. Although I was intrigued and flattered, I couldn't imagine how we could communicate—OK, I could imagine how we could communicate and chose to ignore the invitation. At breakfast the next morning, I wasn't sure how to answer when he asked why I hadn't come to his room so I just smiled, shrugged, and said "Sorry."

Although shops don't open daily until 11am, I found many treasures; mischievous trolls are everywhere and I purchased one for myself. For Joe and Stacy, American friends in Berlin who are getting married, I bought a cheese cutter with a Polar Bear on the handle and a Norwegian wedding card. After asking the word for "birthday", I bought Norwegian birthday cards to give everyone this year. Last year I sent German cards. For a late lunch, I ate at a Pizzeria. I believe it's the best Pizza I've ever had and the atmosphere was intriguing with rafters, walls, ceilings, and shelves displaying an amazing array of artifacts and conversation pieces. My favorite tourist attraction was a Polarium showing a five screen cinema of polar bears, icebergs, glaciers, and vast areas of icy mountains on the Arctic islands of Svalbard. Hungry to learn about this strange land and culture, I went back to the Polarium a second time, especially enjoying the vast wild icy mountain scenes, wishing I could be there but at the same time wanting to be warm, comfortable and safe.

My days were spent walking along the wharf and visiting museums, cathedrals, and shops; every evening I searched the night skies for the fascinating Northern Lights. In my spare time I was able to finish two books, *Desert Flower; the Extraordinary Journey of a Desert Nomad* by Waris Dirie and *The Secret of Shambhala: In Search of the Eleventh Insight* by James Redfield. Finding good books in English is not easy; finding time to read is a rare luxury.

This was one of my favorite trips, I'm realizing how I love traveling solo. I want to return at Winter Solstice when it's dark—totally dark—just to experience what that feels like.

And I'd love to visit the Svalbard Islands in the summer someday, when it's light all night!

From: Carol
To: LittleAli
Subject: **Toe Trouble**
Date: Tuesday, December 12, 2000

I almost had a major back operation—but I chickened out! After three neurosurgeons and a whole slew of other physicians prescribed surgery, I agreed to have it done. However, my surgeon's description to the insurance company caused them to say it was a pre-existing condition and they would not pay. I suppose anything could be considered pre-existing: heart attack because your heart has been gradually getting worse all your life; broken bone because your bones have been deteriorating for years; and my slipped disc and back because I'm getting old and wearing out my body. Actually I think the disc slipped when I fell at Thanksgiving. Although they said it would only cost $15,000, and I could pay that, I decided to wait and have in done in my country where I could communicate easily with my medical team.

The middle toe on my right foot has been looking deformed; actually, dead. Monday evening I went to an orthopedic surgeon, taking all my X-rays and MRI's to get a second opinion. He said my second toe had been broken and was moving over into the third toe, cutting off its circulation. If I had the back operation, it would not help this foot problem, which may be what has caused so many of my problems. He also found bursitis in my hip and gave me three cortisone injections; two in the hip and one at the base of the spine. I look forward to going back next week for another treatment, those shots are amazingly helpful!

That's all the cortisone he can give me without side effects. He also prescribed a new type of orthotics for my shoes.

The toe could have broken when I fell last November; that foot was very painful and did get very swollen and black and blue. Or it might have broken when my desk top fell on it twice the night I moved in.

I took Tuesday off and went to get the prescribed orthotics. Because I begged for an immediate fix, they made temporary changes in my current ones which allowed me to walk out of the office with a livelier step! One of my friends couldn't wear orthotics and needed special shoes. Insurance paid for her to have two pair of custom made shoes. She chose a beautiful pair for dress and full length leather boots with heels. It's nice to know there is an alternative to those with problems orthotics don't fix.

I felt so good I stopped for lunch at KaDeWe (pronounced Caw Dee Vay), the biggest, most wonderful department store in Berlin! In fact, it is the second largest department store in Europe, second only to Harrods of London. The whole top floor (seventh) is a magnificent restaurant/cafeteria with cozy seating arrangements and spectacular views of the city. A multitude of international food varieties are available; making choices was a challenge. KaDeWe is known for having things not available anywhere else in the area, including boxes of baking soda (only tiny packets everywhere else), packets of just add water already sweetened hot chocolate (bitter hot chocolate to cook and add milk everywhere else), and my favorite Gjetost Norwegian cheese.

My feet still felt fabulous, so I went shopping. I'd seen a beautiful hand made dress at a Christmas Market last weekend. Their shop was close, so I stopped in to take a look at these original fashions. For the first time in my life, I paid $250 for a dress! The only colors were dark gray and black. Since Laura had bought a black one, mine had to be different. So mine is gray, two piece, with both the top and the skirt being long and flowing with uneven hems. I just love the way it feels and flows, so I made the big splurge! With mid calf length, long sleeves, and a jewel neck, it can be worn for most any special occasion.

Remember I said I'd like to go back to Tromsø during Winter Solstice? Well, my teaching schedule only allows me to go during Christmas Vacation, so I have booked a flight to be there for New Years' Eve! For a few days, I will see what winter is like in the far North. I'll be in Switzerland again for the rest of Christmas Vacation.

Today I went berserk at work! The networked printer jammed at lunchtime. I was trying to get something printed as a surprise for Lisa and she happened to come in and got on the Internet to print something, which jammed the printer and kept my surprise from printing. At that minute three teachers on other computers decided to print and everything froze. At that moment a bunch of my students needed help and were saying "Ms Coffey….." and teachers were saying, "Why isn't my stuff printing?" and I just got stressed out and said, "Don't anyone print! Nothing is working. Lisa, don't leave. No, Hal (a teacher who just walked in), you can not print! Sorry kids, I have to get this printer fixed." Suddenly everything was quiet; everyone stopped. After about five minutes, I got it working again. I don't think anyone felt mad or hurt, they understood and I think it's fine to show my humanness occasionally, as long as I don't make a habit of it.

Friday I will get my new orthotics, just in time to go with friends to three different Christmas Markets Friday night,

Saturday, and Sunday this weekend here in Berlin. They will all have Glühwein but no sausages or Lebkuchen. Last weekend we were at the Christkindlesmarkt in Nuremburg again, it is definitely the best! I bought all my Christmas gifts, but I can always search for treasures and enjoy the experience.

From: Carol
To: LittleAli
Subject: **Swiss Adventure**
Date: Tuesday, Jan 2, 2001

That New Years' Eve in Tromsø where the sun doesn't shine this time of year DIDN'T HAPPEN! I had to cancel!!! The meniscus in my other knee tore while I was carrying my small suitcase up a long flight of steps in the Kandersteg Train Station. As before, I couldn't put any weight on that leg! I had my trekking pole and used it and the suitcase to get up the steps. A sweet bystander who saw the accident helped me get on the train, which was right at the top of the steps.

Lisa invited me to her New Years Eve Party but Berlin has snow and I was afraid to venture out on my crutches for fear of slipping on the ice and having another accident! What an angel she is! She brought the party to me! We had a wonderful evening with cheese fondue, sect (champagne), and intriguing conversations. Her visitors from Italy, Myscha and David, were very interesting and invited us to visit them this spring. It was a great way to welcome in the New Year with good friends in the comfort of my Berlin home.

For my Christmas Holiday, I went back to Kandersteg, Switzerland. I just don't think there's a better place. Most things were the same as last year, I still stayed in room 333 at Alfa Soleil, the food was still elegant and delicious, and I loved walking through the town daytime and nighttime. The Christmas Eve Service in the little wooden Reform Church was the same, complete with lighted candles on the real trees, but I got there early and didn't sit in the crowded balcony. The other ski area, Sunnbüel, was open this year so I rode the gondola up from town. It is larger; I prefer the smaller ski area where I hiked back to picturesque Oeschinen Lake at the base of the Blüemlisalp. I used my trekking pole everywhere I walked; in town and on the trails. Most people use them even in town, the streets and sidewalks are covered in snow.

Although I went back to Zermatt and saw the Matterhorn again, my favorite trip was by train to Mürren. At Wengen I had to sit in the front of the train to Mürren; the back of the train soon went in a different direction. There can not be a more scenic mountain town than Mürren!!! Steep high majestic mountains totally surround the tiny town built on steep hillsides. To get to the Funicular for a ride up the mountain, I had to walk through Mürren to the tinier town of Gimmelwald. I hadn't heard of this village, but began to realize what a unique place it is, with no cars, no TV's, no food stores; but with plenty of snow, mountains, and cows. The funicular was so steep I felt like I was sitting on stair steps. From there I rode a Gondola to the top of Schilthorn Mountain. Other than the unbelievable 360 degree scenic views, the main attraction there is the Piz Gloria revolving restaurant. Another amazing Swiss architectural achievement, the building turned as I relaxed and enjoyed a bowl of soup and cup of tea while moving mountain panoramas surrounded me; I was totally in my element! This was the area the young couple from Tanzania told me about last year; they did not exaggerate.

Running to catch a train the second day there, I did pull something in my right knee. Consequently, I was cautious, walking straight, careful not to twist the knee, and used my trekking pole everywhere I went, especially on hikes as far as six miles in the snow. How lucky am I to have the meniscus wait to tear as I was leaving instead of any time earlier!

But that trip home was not so good. I was in horrendous pain. Luckily I had valium for emergencies like when my back goes out. I took the valium, then ibuprofen, then another ibuprofen, then a second valium; it barely cut the pain. My reserved seat was many cars from where I boarded the train. I asked the attendant if I could sit somewhere near the door, but she looked at my ticket and sent me on my way. Bearing my full weight as I attempted to get to my seat, my trekking pole broke in two pieces. That got her attention and thankfully she found me a seat close by, helped with my luggage, and reluctantly threw the pole away for me. I did have to go to the bathroom but found I could use the backs of seats as crutches and swing my way through. People were very helpful to move over in their seats when they saw me coming.

Luckily I only had to change trains once—and there was no storm this year. If last year's storm had been this year, I would have been in a hospital at the first stop, or still sitting on that first train! Changing trains in Mannheim, the train attendants got a luggage cart on wheels for my suitcase AND ME! Sitting down on the nearly ground level metal cart was a challenge for my knee and me; pain kept this unique adventure from being the hysterically funny ride it could have been. I sat on the cart, struggled to hold up my feet, and was rolled across to the Berlin train's platform, extremely thankful I didn't have to navigate any stairs! That would have been a bumpy ride! The train trip to

Berlin was uneventful but painful. Although I usually can sleep on trains, and had taken two valium, the pain kept me wide awake for the entire trip.

Arriving in Berlin brought challenges. This time I rode the luggage cart (where were the wheel chairs???) and held my suitcase while the attendant pushed me into a freight elevator for the ride down to ground level. From there he helped me out to a taxi, the driver helped me into my building, and was shocked to see me sit down and scoot up the steps backwards, just like I did with my other knee injury. The difference this time was the crutches waiting for me inside!

The next day, my orthopedic surgeon was ready with his magic injections. I'm still on crutches but able to go anywhere and do most anything again.

From: Carol
To: LittleAli
Subject: **Going to Jenny!**
Date: Thursday, February 8, 2001

Remember Valerie, the teacher who gave me that beautiful black wool coat? She had heard of my medical woes and came to me after Christmas Holiday with the name of her phenomenal physical therapist. Jenny Parkinson is the young woman who helped Valerie get her health turned around and lose all that weight. Valerie gave her such a glowing recommendation; I immediately made an appointment and rushed down to her office. She is half American, half German, and graduated from our school. I have never met a doctor, physical therapist, or any medical worker who understands my body so well! The exercise and treatments she is giving me have helped my back and my walking already. My orthotics are causing the muscles on the bottom of my feet to atrophy, the bottoms of my feet are very tender and I can't even tolerate standing on a carpet barefoot. She said I should go walk barefoot in the sand to build up the muscles, then throw away the orthotics and wear Teva Sandals because they give good arch support and are flexible enough for my feet to work and build muscle too.

So I went to the travel agent and booked a trip to the sandy beaches of the Turkish Rivera for Winter Break starting this weekend. It's a German Package Tour including five days in a 4 star hotel with air fare and ground transportation for only $350. I won't be taking the included German tours; maybe I can find a cute guide instead.

At Jenny's suggestion, I bought an exercise bike to help build up my knees. In case I'm interested, it tells how many kilometers per hour I'm bicycling. My knees are so much better; I hope the crutches won't be needed in Turkey.

Have you heard of a Lymph Drainage (Dra-nauge')? Jenny said I needed one to take the toxins out of my lymphatic system which is in the skin. I had sore spots all over my legs and very itchy ankles with a slight rash. A woman in her office has been specially trained in this procedure. Somewhat similar to a massage but with many differences, she barely touched me in specific paths especially on my extremities, always pushing toward my center. Then she did a pumping motion on my abdomen just above the pelvic bone while telling me to visualize water moving. It reminded me of priming a pump on my grandparents' farm when it had run dry. With instructions to drink lots of water, take a hot bath in Epsom salts, and return for nine more sessions, I went home to enthusiastically follow her instructions. The strangest thing happened; I had a lot of dirty water bowel movements with no pain and very little warning. I think it was all the toxins lurking under my skin. The next day I had no itching ankles and no tender spots on my legs either. I only went back for one more treatment. She had an accident and was not able to continue the treatments, and I felt she had already healed me.

It's good to be feeling better. Friday night I went to dinner with friends and Saturday Lisa and I went downtown to see *The Legend of Bagger Vance*. Since one of my trekking poles broke on the Swiss trip, I bought a new pair on Saturday. These are much sturdier and have a spring in them. Hopefully I'll be hiking up mountains again soon. Hey, I can't believe you're planning a hiking trip in the Pyrenees! You're such a mountain woman!

We had a snow and ice storm Monday morning. I was ready to leave for work when Chris, my principal, called and said it was too slick for me to come in. He was concerned I might fall again and have another injury. Such personal concern I get here!

Luckily the snow and ice had melted by afternoon and I went for my last knee injection. It was a series of three Hyaluronan injections* in both knees; a gel like substance which supplements the synovial fluid in my knees. It's extremely expensive but better than surgery. When they ordered the injections, I received a bill for $8000 in the mail. Of course it arrived on a Friday after their office had closed for the weekend. I was so upset all weekend; I made a pact with myself to only open bills when their office is open.** Early Monday morning I was relieved to learn that was not a bill, but a statement of all they had ordered. I would only be receiving a small portion of that shipment. Why oh why did they send that to me?????

Friday I bought a little camera. The one I have is so large I hesitate to carry it on my trips. This little one will be convenient; I will have no more excuses. With no idea where to find a camera store, I rode the bus to Steglitz, a rather large shopping area, looked across the street, saw the word *Phono*, and found cameras in the window. Seeing nothing less than $200, I asked for the cheapest one that zoomed; the clerk showed me this one for $60. It's just what I needed.

Laura and I made reservations for a cruise down the Nile in Egypt during Spring Break with a British Singles group. Language should not be a barrier on this cruise.

---

* Those injections worked so well, I had Synvisc injections of synovial fluid at home in 2005 and 2009, I think that is about the same thing. Although only expected to last six months, their cushioning effect on my knees has held up very well for me.

** To this day, I will not open a bill if offices are not open. In case of an error or a question, I want to be able to call immediately.

From: Carol
To: LittleAli
Subject: **Turkish Riviera**
Date: Monday, February 19, 2001

I just got back from a week in Paradise on the Turkish Riviera along the Mediterranean Sea! Surrounded by sunshine and warmth, it really really felt good to walk in the sand and water. Temperatures were in the high 60's and low 70's; not bad for winter. My luxurious 4-star hotel was on the beach with amazing views of the sea, several pools, and palm trees from my balcony. The sound of the waves and the cool ocean breeze, especially at night, made for a very restful sleep. Walking barefoot about a mile every day in the clean white sand has healed my thin-skinned wimpy-muscled tender feet. Jenny was right!

Arriving in Turkey a week ago Saturday, my first task was to get a Visa stamp for my passport before leaving the airport. A colleague who makes frequent trips to Turkey said the Visa stamp would cost about $25, the travel agent said it would be $45, my Turkish guidebook said it would not cost anything; I paid $50 and wondered what criteria was used for this required stamp. My next task was to find Oger Tours where they led me to bus 41: a big white, very comfortable, air conditioned van. All the occupants (German) and the Turkish driver and guide were quite nice and helpful. At the first hotel, I asked to get out and take a picture of the beautiful tropical flowers in bloom and was surprised the guide understood English. Giving permission in English, he then added that maybe we could get together later. I thought that was interesting and that I may have misunderstood, but said, "maybe we can."

After a 90 minute ride in a continually empting van, we arrived at my hotel. The guide, Mustafa, (pronounced Moo stall' fuh), took my suitcase in, then "cornered" me and asked if he could see me during the week. Since I had considered hiring a guide who spoke English and had no idea where to find one, I said, "Well, I do need a guide, how much do you charge?" "No money, just Petrol." OK, gas was expensive, about four times what it costs in the U.S., but a guide would charge for that and much more. He agreed to pick me up at 2 pm the next day and take me to his home town, Alanya, a city on my list of places to visit. Before he left I asked if I could give him a tip, he said "Not me, but you can give a tip to the bus driver." I gave the driver a small tip; I was still confused about the money. Soon I learned to drop six zeros and multiply by three to get Deutschmarks. From there I knew my way around. Basically, 15-million Turkish Lira was 45 DM, or about $22.

I could tell Mustafa was young and seemed quite nice; I liked his eyes and smile and thought he would be a good guide. I know women, even old women, traveling alone need to be cautious, but since I knew who he worked for and my hotel staff knew him; it seemed pretty safe.

Driving into the hotel, the ocean was not visible. Coming in from the back, we maneuvered around potholes and construction barriers. Seeing my room for the first time, it looked simple enough with two small beds, until the porter pulled back the curtains and opened the sliding glass doors. I let out a scream of delight and ran to the balcony. What an amazing view of the sea and sandy beach and two dramatically shaped swimming pools and palm trees and flowers and bushes in bloom. Paradise!

Dinner was an incredible buffet of a variety of unknown delicacies. The maitre de seated me with a German woman who was very sweet but didn't speak any English. I would have preferred sitting alone, but I'm sure he thought he was doing me a favor. The German lady and I uncomfortably attempted communication and she was extremely gracious throughout the meal. Later I walked along the beach by myself. I loved the sound of the waves, the amazingly bright stars, and the warm air!

Sunday:
Sunday was my 58th birthday and will probably be the most memorable birthday of my life. Breakfast was another amazing buffet with seating in bright sunshine on the terrace. I couldn't find a fork, knife, or napkin and could not communicate that to the waiter, so I ate my tomatoes, cucumbers, Feta cheese, and olives with my fingers and used my Kleenex as a napkin. It worked. After breakfast, I walked barefoot about a mile along the beach and waded in the cold waves. The sand was white and very soft on my feet; there were no seashells or debris of any kind. They must have beach sweepers like we have street sweepers. Later I lay on the beach for a chilly two hours until time to get ready for the trip to Alanya at 2 pm.

Being a bit cautious, I left a note in my room including Mustafa's name, cell phone (A Cell phone is called a *Handy* in Germany and in Turkey too), place of work, work phone, and where we were going. A friend of his was driving his new used car. Mustafa sat in the back seat with me, in the middle, with his arm around me; I guess he thought that was romantic. His friend had just washed his car so the back seat was wet, it took me awhile to realize but when I got out of the car, I had a wet seat. We laughed; they teased me just as anyone would in America, and Mustafa gave me his jacket to put around my waist until it dried. The guys were a lot of fun and took me about 30 minutes away to their home town, Alanya, a beautiful small city on a peninsula in the Mediterranean Sea below the Taurus Mountains. We visited a castle, a tower, and ruins of the old city wall, took some pictures of each other; then took a tour of mosques, minarets, and the historic city. I can't remember all the rulers and countries that inhabited the area, but it has a fascinating political history, including rendezvous' of Anthony and Cleopatra. It was interesting and especially meaningful being with local young people having a fun day in Turkey. I didn't feel like a tourist—rather a guest.

Mustafa took me into an underground cave; I paid for me but he got in free. It must be a custom that locals are seen as guides and tourists pay. This cave was beautiful with the standard stalactite and stalagmite formations, but it also had water. Mustafa said people come here to soak in the healing warm water to eliminate arthritis and other pains. It was humid and not a place I would want to spend much time since I like fresh air and wide open spaces.

For lunch, they took me to a "fast food" café: tables and chairs on a grassy lawn of what looked like someone's home. They ordered a homemade flat bread like a tortilla with little green things, interesting and pretty tasty. I'm sorry I couldn't understand when they told me what it is called. The guys drank their usual drink—yogurt with water and some salt. I took a taste; it seemed much like buttermilk, which I like on occasion, but not on this hot day in the sun. Since I was afraid to drink the water, I ordered the nearly universal drink, coca cola. I paid for the meal and of course for the Petrol. It is obvious they do not have much money, but very sweet of them to take a day to show a foreigner around.

Wanting to show me their favorite picnic spot and water hole, they took me up a beautiful canyon with a turquoise colored river which is spanned by a very high bridge. A hammock had been strung high under the bridge and that is where they dive into the river! Very ingenious, probably dangerous, definitely thrilling, but not something I would ever try.

We stopped at a beautiful old restaurant made of stone with many small rooms and only pillows on the floor for seating.

Food was cooked at an open fireplace by a woman sitting on a pillow, antiques hung from rafters and some gifts were sold in an adjoining shop. I bought an elegant hand thrown pottery bowl decorated with burlap and the traditional Turkish Evil Eye good luck charm. Mustafa said Turkish people usually sit on pillows. The guys drank their traditional yogurt drink, I had a coke. They don't drink alcohol because their Muslim religion forbids it. Otherwise they seemed to lead a European lifestyle.

Back in town, his friend dropped us off at the market where Mustafa's car was parked. He shares a very old Mercedes with his family. He is 32, divorced, and lives with his parents and three brothers; only he and another brother are working. The family used to take tourists out on their small boat until it sank four years ago; they don't have the money to buy another yet. It was Sunday and we visited an outdoor market filled with locals. Feeling like the only tourist, I really enjoyed seeing that piece of local culture and felt privileged to be there. Huge displays of fruit, vegetables, and practical cotton clothes were the main products. Mustafa bought me a fake rose for Valentines Day. I told him today was my birthday (didn't say which one) so I would think of the rose as a birthday gift but he bought me the traditional Turkish Evil Eye good luck piece on a safety pin for my birthday gift. He said the eye makes evil stay away from me. I like to think it means the eye of God is watching over and protecting me.

He found his parents at the market and drove them home in the family car which he was borrowing to take me to my hotel. His parents were really sweet, spoke some English, and gave me figs and peanuts in the shell. His family lives in an apartment near the town center.

When he took me to my hotel, I invited him to have dinner with me there. Somehow that seemed more pleasant than being seated with the gracious German women again, each of us trying unsuccessfully to communicate. My meals are included, so I expected to pay extra for his. However, they would not let me, maybe because he is a local guide. All meals are huge buffets with an incredible variety of meats and fresh olives, vegetables, fruits and breads. I thrived on the tomatoes, cucumbers, Feta cheese and a variety of olives; breakfast and dinner! Mustafa said that is what most Turkish people eat every day. I would love that; the tomatoes tasted homegrown, the cucumbers were the long narrow ones grown locally and were never bitter. I have never had olives that were so succulent and not at all soggy. We walked on the beach after dinner, I loved being out there, but he was interested in being romantic. Since I wasn't interested; he accepted that and soon went home.

His English is not real good—but better than most. He's very neat, clean, educated (tourism school degree after high school), is nice looking and had a good sense of humor. Sometimes it's so hard to communicate though—mostly feelings and ideas are lost—which can be draining. He wanted to see me everyday, but I needed space and relaxation. I only saw him Sunday, Monday, and Thursday.

Monday:

Monday was such a beautiful morning! I hadn't realized how much I missed the sun and blue skies while in Berlin. I think the sea is very healing too. I felt wonderful all day Sunday. I didn't use the crutch at all, not even when climbing rocks and uneven natural stepping stone steps. Mustafa was always there with a helping hand but I rarely needed it. My knees didn't hurt at all.

At breakfast I chose a seat on the patio; that nice German woman invited me to join her and her friends but I motioned to my patio seat. Later, after walking barefoot on the beach and lying in the sun on the cold windy beach, I tried one of the pools, hoping for warmth. The friendly German woman saw me and said it was warmer by the fake rocks where she and her friends were. There was an extra chair and she brought me a pad; I had wondered where those were kept. She is such a gracious person, wish I understood her better.

At 1 pm I went in to get ready for another adventure with Mustafa at 2 pm. He brought the family car, we promptly ran out of gas somewhere before Manavgat. He didn't seem surprised, just got the plastic can from the trunk and left me sitting there with Turkish music playing on the car radio. I took a picture of a beautiful Mosque in the distance and just sat and soaked up the peaceful surroundings. Two young women stopped to ask for money but I had no Turkish money; Mustafa had all my change for the gas. When I explained, she smiled and walked on. When Mustafa returned, he said they were gypsies.

On the road again, we stopped at an ATM in Manavgat where I got $75 worth of Turkish money, then went to the gas station. I told him to fill the tank, but he didn't understand, so I only paid $15. We stopped to see beautiful waterfalls and checked out the tourist markets where I bought a gorgeous green rayon pants suit and a few table scarves in Turkish rug designs.

Our next stop was Side (pronounced Sea' duh), an ancient village built on a peninsula in the Mediterranean Sea surrounded by historic ruins from as far back as the seventh century BC. My favorite ruin was a coliseum-like theater built in 2AD seating 17,000. He gave me an historical tour complete with stories of wild animal combats, naval battles reenacted in the water-filled orchestra pit, gladiator fights, slavery sales, slaves thrown to animals, and even church services during the 5th and 6th century under Dionysus. Side is a bustling seaport town with festive markets and sea-side cafes; an interesting contrast of ancient and contemporary side by side.

At a market in Side center, I bought a small delicate white tablecloth with hand made flower embroidered designs, a pair of leg length wool socks hand knitted with Turkish designs for Erin, and some Turkish-rug-looking bookmarks. Merchants were pretty aggressively wanting my patronage, but when Mustafa held my hand, they left me alone.

Down by the harbor we ate in a quaint café outside near the water. I ordered lamb kabob and the wonderful tomato, cucumber, feta cheese salad and a coke. Mustafa ordered the same but had tea; he doesn't drink coke either. I should lead such a healthy lifestyle! Strangely, I think he wanted fish but ordered what I ordered. I tried to explain he could order what he wanted, but I don't think he understood. I was paying, but I didn't care what he ordered and I don't think the fish cost more than the lamb. Several cats joined us for dinner; it seemed like a natural occurrence. Once I dropped a piece of food and Mustafa jumped to pick it up. He said, "5 minute rule" and I was surprised this custom was so universal. I didn't eat it though.

On our way home, we stopped for a walk on the beach. The night was dark but beautiful, a storm was coming, it was high tide, and waves were rolling in fast. Driving back, I asked about Turkish customs, especially Muslim (they say Moo' slum) traditions. It seems they are very relaxed in Western Turkey, are more traditional in Eastern

Turkey, but are much more rigorous in Iraq, Iran, Tunisia, etc. In Turkey, women have the same say as men; many don't wear the traditional head coverings, they can choose. Coming in on the plane, I sat with a young Turkish woman and her daughter. I asked her why she was not wearing the head covering and she said "Don't want to." Mustafa says Istanbul is another world and you will find all customs there. I asked why he was so nice to me when his country does not like my country. He said his people don't like my government but they do like our people. I thought that was a nice sentiment and was certainly the way I felt as I traveled and met the people.

Sitting in the car at a Video store where I hoped to purchase a romantic Turkish male vocal CD like I'd been hearing on his radio all day, we briefly continued our Turkish customs discussion. He said "Turkish men have all been circumcised; they don't do that in America, do they?" I informed him that many American men were circumcised also. Then he asked, "Have you ever seen a Turkish man's penis?" Trying to not appear shocked, I calmly said "No, I haven't." He enthusiastically answered, "I show you one!!!" I laughed and said "No, no, no!" and got out of the car, escaping to the safety of the Video store where he helped me select just the right CD.

When we arrived at my hotel, he asked to see me again Tuesday. I told him I needed alone time. He suggested several other trips and dancing at night, but I just couldn't commit to anything right then. I had explained there was no future for us but he was trying to get me to come back in July, my next unscheduled vacation; I stated that obviously I was too old for him but he countered that age doesn't matter, what's in the heart is what matters. He is very romantic but frankly, I don't feel any chemistry, thank goodness! Truthfully, I don't believe a 32 year old man would have a sincere interest in a 58 year old woman other than money or maybe a Green Card to the U.S. I have heard of gigolos, maybe he's trying to be one; well, that's not working.

It seems I'm the only American anywhere around here, and the only American to come on Oger Tours in the four years Mustafa has worked there. The waiters did seem surprised I was from America. It's amazing to think I may have been the only American traveling in Southern Turkey at the time, and maybe the only tourist traveling solo. Most tourists are German. There are American tours there starting in May through the summer but, according to Mustafa, never anyone traveling alone! I had no idea I was such a phenomenon; it felt good.

Tuesday:
Monday night's storm came in with a vengeance. Palm trees were swinging, waves were beating the shore, lightening was flashing, thunder was roaring, and the wind was so strong I had to close my balcony door to sleep. Tuesday morning's sunrise announced the storm was over, all was calm and serene again. It felt good to have no agenda; to walk barefoot a mile on the cool beach in the newly washed air while rougher than usual waves played catch with my feet.

My hotel was not near any cities, it was at the end of a long string of huge luxurious hotels on the beach. Empty fields were next to our building. Wanting to explore, I walked down the road and turned into a little dirt street which, to my surprise, led to a whole village! There was a big market place with several dirt streets of shops. Of course the vendors were begging me to look at their treasures. I seemed to be the only tourist in the whole village! I bought a few little things; some onyx and a necklace* threaded with wooden discs for 50 cents.

A young man at a gold jewelry shop took me to his mother's linen shop when I said I was looking for a tablecloth. I had planned to look for a big tablecloth for mother's new dining room table. Her work looked perfect, with cutwork flowers, white on white, elegant! While I was looking at the biggest one on display, she said she had more in the back. Using German and hand gestures, I asked for the largest she had in white or off-white. She came out with one that was four meters long, we bargained for the price, and I bought my mother an heirloom handmade tablecloth. Hope it fits.**

The mother, teenage daughter, and grandfather offered me black tea or hot apple juice. I chose the tea. It took awhile and was scalding hot when served, so I felt it was definitely safe to drink. Tea was served in a very small clear, extremely delicate glass with no handle, very narrow and a little tall, along with a glass saucer. Later, I was served tea in a similar manner in other places so it must be traditional. Cubes of sugar and a tiny spoon were always included. They were so gracious, we communicated in German, hand gestures, smiles, and laughter. The adult son, who spoke a little English, joined us for tea. After tea, they all worked to find me matching placemats. I bought 12 for 50 cents each. I also found navy blue pillow covers to cover my red and green couch pillows. They were hand embroidered in gold thread; the mother showed me how she does the elegant hand work.

The village fascinated me; I had never seen such a place. I wandered the dirt streets and paths. At home we would say there were living in poverty, but everyone had a big smile, seemed very relaxed and I believe they were quite happy, living an idyllic lifestyle in their houses made of anything they could find, pieced together however they could. Although materialistically in poverty, basic needs were met and there was no poverty of the heart. I wondered if duct tape was used, but decided it was probably too modern and expensive for these dwellings. The dirt yards were inhabited by cows, goats, and chickens; so milk, cheese, yogurt, butter, and meat were readily available without the antibiotics and other additives that we are used to.

A teenage boy peeked over a fence covered in Bougainvillea, the delicate tropical flowers that grow so prolifically here. He asked if I'd like to enter the mosque. I had no idea that little building was a mosque, but I said "Yes, I would." His English was quite good; he gave me plastic bags to put over my shoes because I said I couldn't go without their support. I was surprised my head did not need to be covered. He sprinkled a lot of perfume on my hand and showed me pictures of people putting it on their hands, head, faces; anywhere. Thank goodness it didn't smell bad, as he kept sprinkling it on me. After entering and viewing the mosque, he asked if I'd like to go up into the minaret. I hadn't noticed that either, but it was a very tall, thin structure just outside. When he handed me a big, very dim, flashlight, I began to be skeptical. Opening the door, he motioned for me to climb the extremely narrow winding steps. Seeing that he had two club feet, I realized he did not intend to go up there himself. I could see darkness would be total until I got to the tiny window at the top, realized this was a perfect place for spiders and other creepy crawly creatures, changed my mind and returned the flashlight, with gratitude and thanks. He showed me where I could give a donation if I wanted, and of course I was happy to contribute. Later I asked Mustafa if people usually went up into minarets and he said no; I can certainly see why. I'm thinking no one has been in that one for years!

Later, I took my camera back for pictures of the woman and daughter to show my mother who made her table cloth. Being careful not to be obnoxious or even obvious and not to include people, I also captured pictures of purple bougainvillea, orange and lemon trees, some of the homes, farm animals in the yards, and the mosque and minaret. One restaurant owner wanted me to take his picture, but I declined. I expected he would expect money, as I had learned in Nepal, and he just wasn't that picturesque. After the very warm trek to and from the village twice, a stroll on the cool windy beach was the perfect antidote.

Wednesday:
I checked with Oger Tours Wednesday about my free bus tour to Antalya Thursday. They said it leaves at 7:40 am and returns late afternoon. Thinking that was too long, I said I wouldn't be going. But later I was reading about what was there and decided I'd like to go, especially to look for a Turkish rug and maybe a gold necklace, which I had researched and hoped to purchase on this trip. I often regret not buying a Tibetan rug in Nepal; I thought I didn't have the money. Mustafa had asked to take me but I said I didn't like cities. I called Mustafa to see if he was the guide on that trip. No, he wasn't but he could ride free and show me around. I called Oger Tours again to sign up but they had already filled my space. Calling Mustafa again, he suggested we go in his car at 9am, which sounded good to me. Feeling like I was taking advantage of him, I made the decision to give him a tip equal to the cost of hiring a guide for the time he spent with me. The cost of Petrol and meals just didn't cover wear and tear on the family car, not to mention the value of his time. I didn't want to be a

stingy, greedy American; I wanted to be a gracious, generous American; a good representative of my country.

I spent the day walking on the beach, sunbathing by the pool, and reading. Luxury is good for a short time, but I'm just not the type to sit around much. At least I got 18 postcards written and mailed. The stamps here must be licked but are still better quality than in Germany where I lick them and they still need to be glued.

This place filled up Wednesday! German and French tourists came in droves; it was the beginning of the summer season! Can you imagine, summer begins February 15th in that part of the world? I was still the only English speaking person and also the only person traveling alone! Cool! There are single women traveling together, but no men without women.

The hotel shops opened for the season. I found a beautiful 14 Karat (US measure) white gold necklace I love. It's longer than I wanted (48 cm) so I must wait until it's shortened. Although I usually prefer silver and have no gold jewelry, I have a few outfits that look better with gold. Since Turkey is known for good quality gold, I thought it was the place to buy one.

Thursday:
At 9am Thursday, Mustafa arrived for our trip to Antalya. It was a really sweet, special day. What better way to tour and explore than with someone driving me wherever I want, stopping whenever I want, patiently waiting while I shop, being wonderful company—friendly, fun, laughing, talking in English, and also protective, always carrying all my things, being sure I get the right change, getting me better deals, and translating for me? This time I made sure

he totally filled the gas tank in the morning and at the end of the day too.

Parking on a small back street in a residential section, we walked to historical buildings, a clock tower, a castle, aqueduct, ancient city walls, and mosques. Not wanting to go inside, I preferred a quick sight-seeing tour this time. On to the fantastic marketplace in the Old Town, we walked along narrow winding cobblestone streets with very old crumbling picturesque stone and wood shops. Wares were hanging and displayed everywhere; vendors were calling to me from all sides. Mustafa protected me some; I'm pretty good at saying "No" too. He found me a wonderful carpet store; we went in, sat on the couch, and were treated to a grand colorful display of Turkish Rugs. I knew what I wanted and with a quick glance, pointed one out. The salesman held it up, put it on the floor in front of us, let me check it out, showed me how it looks different from two directions, and said this one was silk and cotton. The others are wool, thicker, and not shiny and delicate. His English was good and Mustafa only needed to translate a few times. However, he and the salesman often spoke in Turkish; I would have liked to know what they were saying. After looking at one more, I made my choice. Then we were served very hot apple tea in the traditional tiny glass cups with saucers, spoons and sugar cubes, and the bargaining began. The initial price was 1600 DM, then a very special price for first day of the season, first customer of the day, 1300 DM. I got up and said I would be looking around in other shops and may come back later in the day. He asked what price I could afford, I said 800 DM; he talked about business and needing to sell etc. His best price was 850 DM ($386); I agreed, and he folded the approximately 4' x 6' carpet*** into a tight package small enough to fit into my suitcase! I paid 10 million lira ($34) with cash and the rest with a credit card. Mustafa said I bargained well but said he had no idea how much they were worth. Somehow I doubted that, and also thought he should be getting a percentage, maybe that $34 cash for bringing me in there. On other trips in other countries, our guides would ask us to tell the cashier what tour we were on; they received a percentage. I didn't see the cash change hands this time and wondered how it worked here.

Continuing through quaint Old Town shops, I found a few little treasures in a very short time. We quickly checked shops where gold jewelry was sold, I wanted to compare their prices to the one I was planning to buy, and was relieved to see that my price was a good one, probably because I had bargained. We had delicious pizza for lunch at an outdoor café on the harbor with fishing boats—and a castle above the aqueducts above us and I got locked in a toilet! I said I needed to go to the toilet and I hoped it was a Western one because my knee injury would make it difficult for me to use an Eastern one, which are holes in the floor and my knees didn't allow me to squat. He said if I didn't come back he'd come to help. That was a joke—and a premonition! Luckily it was a Western style toilet. I hoped the water on the floor was from a recent cleaning. I could not get that door to unlock and open to let me out! I tried everything I could think of. It must have been 10 minutes. Amazingly, I was not claustrophobic and did not panic. I knew I could pound on the door and call for help (hilfe, bitte) in German, someone would probably help. But finally with a very strong pull and just the right turn of the lock and then a gentle push, it miraculously opened.

While walking through the harbor looking at the boats, a gypsy woman approached Mustafa and in Turkish asked to read our palms and tell our fortune. Although he kept telling her we were not interested, she followed and badgered us in a loud voice, much worse than any male vendor I have encountered.

We could have taken a one hour boat ride to a ski mountain out in the Mediterranean Sea, but I chose not to. After a quick walking tour through New Town, Mustafa found me a huge open market. I was looking for a dress or outfit, but all the clothing laying on big tables was very plain, functional, high quality cotton, low prices, but not my style. They were exactly Mustafa's style. I suddenly felt drained of energy, sat down, ordered a coke, and offered to buy Mustafa a drink. He declined and would sit with me, but I told him I wanted to buy him an outfit if he would like, and handed him some cash. He seemed happy to do that and soon came back with a well coordinated outfit of slacks, a sport shirt, and a cotton sweater. He is a very neat dresser and that will be a good look for work or anywhere else. I couldn't believe he could get so much for such a small amount of money!

As we walked back to the car, I realized I needed to visit another toilet. Yuk! He found me a public one in the center which was ok, but the attendant gave me a tiny bit of paper to take in. Luckily I always carry tissues with me. Mustafa paid the fee so I don't know what it cost, but it was a clean Western toilet and I was thankful.

Walking back through the tiny alleys, we found the car and started driving down a main street. Suddenly Mustafa turned down an alley. I said, "You know all the shortcuts, don't you?" The streets got more narrow, he barely missed a parked car, then a man in a passing car had to fold in his side mirror; Mustafa couldn't get his to fold. With no scratches and no scrapes, we continued to the most narrow place on what looked like a dead end street, pulled next to a building, and he said, "Do you need a toilet?" I said no, he said "I do." and got out and ran into the back of a restaurant, staying about 15 minutes. While we were meandering down the back streets, I was thinking we were in the area of the carpet shop. Waiting in the car, I was pretty sure he was going back to that shop to get the $34 cash I had paid. I'll never know if I'm right because I didn't want to embarrass him by asking. I hope he did get that money.

While waiting in the car, some vehicles came from what I thought was a dead end. At first they were small and were able to slowly inch past Mustafa's very old Mercedes while I held my breath and smiled. I wasn't worried, just watching the scene. The drivers didn't seem at all upset. Then a tractor pulling a big wagon came around that corner. I knew he was too big to get through and was curious to see what came next. The driver got out and looked at me; I threw up my hands, shrugged, and rolled down the window. He asked where the driver was, I said "Toilet" and pointed at the restaurant. He walked up and down the street and talked to all the men standing around watching. To me, it was very comical but I tried to keep a straight face. Actually no one seemed to be upset. Mustafa had left the keys in the car, it was a stick shift and I wouldn't dare try to drive it. Looking around, I could see there was no place it could be moved out of the way, there was no room!!! After much consideration, the driver decided to try. With the help of one of the men, he slowly moved, inch by inch, through the narrow space. When the wagon was beside the car, it was at a bad angle and the back was getting too close. The mirror would be the first point of contact. Remembering Mustafa had not been able to get his mirror folded in earlier, I decided to give it a try anyway and I prayed. With much effort and prayer, I got that mirror to fold in at the very last second and the wagon got by without a scratch! With a lot of relief and a bit of pride, I relaxed and waited. As soon as that tractor was out of sight, Mustafa happily emerged from the restaurant. The men standing around told him about the tractor, everyone was laughing. Getting in the car, he seemed exceptionally happy, but also calm and unshaken, like this was an everyday occurrence. He was able to unfold the mirror and backed through the entire alley and another side street, inch by inch. Crazy! And he didn't seem to think I'd done anything out of the ordinary, I wonder if he would have been upset if I hadn't been able to fold it in? Probably not, he seemed very even tempered and always in a good mood.

When we got back, he asked to see me Friday. With a 2 am departure Saturday morning, I just wanted a restful day on Friday. Asking me to send pictures of our trips, he gave me his home address. I already had his "handy" number, and when he asked for my phone number, I gave it to him but didn't give him my address. Explaining how much I appreciated his assistance, I gave him the tip, which he accepted with thanks.

Friday:

After my traditional delightful breakfast Friday morning, I walked another mile barefoot on the beach. It was so cold I wore a warm jacket and lycra tights under my cargo pants. Getting my bare feet in the water got my pants wet; I felt exhilarated and wanted to dance like Zorba the Greek, but decided to appear civilized. I was the only person wading in the cold water. A young Turkish man came along and invited me to a Disco that night. I said "I'm leaving tonight." He spoke good English; we talked and walked. He could tell I am American and said there are no other Americans around there, just Germans and some French. I said "and Turkish." and he laughed. I walked back in the water.

Before going to Turkey, I had heard that Americans were not welcome there, as their government was not happy with our government at that time. Consequently I did not tell many people where I was from. When they asked, I usually said "English." If they asked more, I'd say "London." Only a few knew my true origin.

Stopping in the jewelry shop for my necklace, I nervously signed the credit card receipt for 78-million Turkish Lira, but calmed myself with the fact that I was only paying $114 for the first gold necklace of my life.

Back in my room, I counted my remaining Lira and made deposits in tip boxes at the restaurant, bar, reception desk, and in an envelope in my room. Not wanting to leave with Lira, I spent it all. Deutschmarks are accepted nearly everywhere here, so I knew I would have money for the bus driver's tip. With much relief and a bit of disbelief, I was able to get my suitcase closed with a whole Turkish carpet and other purchases inside.

Saturday: At 2 am Saturday, I was the only person leaving my hotel. Although the bus was empty, the guide said I had to sit with him. As the tour bus filled with 22 other tourists for our 90 minute trip, I realized everyone else came in pairs; I was the odd one. The guide could speak English, which he learned from black market DVD's of American movies with Turkish subtitles. He spoke German to the group, then took my suitcase and backpack and told me to come with him. Maybe because of my crutch, maybe because I'm an American, maybe because he's heard Americans are good tippers, I was escorted into the airport and taken to my boarding line. The Antalya airport is well marked in English and has very clean Western toilets. My flight on Sun Express, a charter company, was comfortable; there was no first class, but they did have a smoking section. I haven't seen a smoking section on an airline for about 20 years. Thankfully I was in row five ahead of the smoke and did not notice it. Breakfast was German lunchmeat—I missed my Turkish breakfasts.Landing in Germany was so funny—I'm on a plane full of Germans in a charter plane. When Berlin came into view through thick clouds, it was very gray, looked like it was raining (it wasn't) and we knew the temperature was basically freezing. Everyone moaned—in unison! My sentiments exactly! We'd all just been to Paradise, basking in the warm sunshine and fresh sea air. This was the first time I've traveled exclusively with Germans. They cheer and clap their hands when the plane lands! Sweet!

I'm so glad this is Presidents' Day, and we don't return to school until tomorrow, I needed time to unwind and refocus.

---

* I wore that necklace quite often until it broke in 2010.
**Mother's tablecloth was a perfect fit and has been used for many family feasts.
*** I have really enjoyed using my Turkish Rug everywhere I've lived and it still looks perfect in 2010.

From: Carol
To: LittleAli
Subject: **Pictures of Paradise**
Date: Saturday, February 24, 2001

Pictures from my trip to Turkey are finally processed. I had a little trouble with the reprints. For some reason, I was not as careful writing the numbers as I am with my checking account. When I asked for eleven reprints of the best pictures, they only sent two. It took awhile, but as I looked at my numbers and tried to think in German, I saw the eleven (| |) I had written as vertical marks like we do at home, as two tally marks in German. Without the little flag on the top left (11), those straight marks we use are just marks. So I asked for nine more reprints, picked them up yesterday, and you can expect some pictures in the mail when they get there.

I'll send Mustafa the ones he's in too, as he asked. He has called a couple of times, sweet but short; I'm sure it's pretty expensive to make those calls. Although he keeps asking me to come in July when I quit work, I continue to say I won't be going back. Times like this, I wish I had caller ID.

On March 5, I will be doing an In-service Computer Training for the teachers in our building. Right now I'm preparing the information packet which must be detailed and easy for them to understand and use after the training. Being basically lazy, I can't seem to get my head in gear to get focused, organized, and concentrate on doing it! Going into the session, demonstrating, and teaching will be easy; but doing that packet—not a piece of cake!

What a beautiful day here! About four inches of wet snow fell last night. This morning the sun came out and the snow on everything really lifted my spirits. I took pictures and walked around the neighborhood admiring how everything looked so fresh and new! This may be the last snow I ever see in Berlin; sadly my time here is coming to an end, but happily I'll be seeing you in late July.

From: Carol
To: LittleAli
Subject: **Egyptian Cruise**
Date: Thursday, May 3, 2001

Life has been good here. From Saturday, Apr 14 until the 21st, I was cruising down the Nile in Egypt. After flying home, I re-packed, and spent the next week sunbathing on the Mediterranean in Tunisia. Sometimes I have to pinch myself, is this really real?

My Egyptian trip was so filled with wondrous amazing sights and activities; I can hardly remember when and where everything happened. Relaxing in Tunisia the next week may have cleared my mind of important details, but here's how I remember Egypt:

The Egyptian Cruise began in London where Laura and I met ten British Singles from the tour group (*Solos Holidays*) we'd be traveling with, and two of her friends from the United States who were our roommates on this trip. We flew into Luxor and stayed in a luxurious hotel Saturday night. When driving at night, I was surprised to see that most vehicles on the road did not use their headlights until almost passing a car, if at all. Although it was dark, there seemed to be some ambient light, possibly reflections from the white sands, like we sometimes have from winter snows. The light colored cars were easy to see. Later I asked our guide why drivers didn't use their headlights at night. He said it was to keep the bulbs from burning out so fast. For myself, I would choose safety over economy!

Sunday morning we toured the Temple of Luxor and the complex of Karnak. The tour guide kept a fast moving pace as he explained the history and meaning of the murals, ancient carvings and statues, with special attention to the fertility aspects of the people. He kept saying "Yella, yella." and we soon learned that meant "Hurry, hurry!" in his language. Although everything was interesting, standing around is much more difficult for my back and legs than walking; the sun was hot, the cement was hard, and my mind wandered back in time to what life was like for the people who lived there so long ago. Luxor is the ancient city of Thebes and the ruins of the temples and complex of Karnak are within the current modern city, creating a distinct contrast of the ancient and contemporary cultures.

The famous Valley of the Kings and Valley of the Queens are just across the Nile River, but we had to wait until our return to Luxor on Friday before touring these famous burial grounds. It was fascinating to learn that the dead could only be buried on the West side of the river Nile

Sunday afternoon we boarded our riverboat, *The Soleil*, and began our fantastic cruise down the Nile River to the small town of Edfu. Although much smaller than the big cruise ships, we had all the comforts, including a large dining room, a snack bar on deck, a swimming pool, several shops, a gathering room for our parties, and beautiful river views from our individual air-conditioned rooms.

On the first night, we were told we would be expected to dress in gallebayas for a Gallebaya Party later in the week. I thought that was a good way to help the local economy, as we were taken to many markets where beautiful varieties of these colorful traditional floor length dresses for women and men were sold. Most of the men dress in western clothing now but about a fourth still wear the gallebaya. We saw very few women on our trip, so I'm not sure how they dress. The one I chose is royal blue with short sleeves, a V-neck, and beautiful gold trim. Made of high quality soft Egyptian cotton, it is very comfortable and will probably be my summer robe for years.*

Before we were turned loose in the markets, our guide informed us of the boundaries. In the outdoor markets, we were not to go in the back. We were safe from the men (there were no women) as long as we were in the open, but we must not go in their closed off areas regardless of how much we were encouraged or cajoled. The vendors, on the other hand, were not allowed to cross the chalk line in front of their stalls. Each morning a rifle-carrying guard drew a line in chalk along the front of the booths. The vendors could speak or call to us but could not cross the line. If we were within the line, they could bribe, bargain, flirt, or use any verbal means to get us to buy their products. Rifle-carrying guards patrolled the area all day. Such strict rules gave me cause to use extra caution while traveling in this country.

Our guide also told us to keep money we'd need for the day in one place, and our other money and valuables out of sight. I wore a money belt around my waist under my clothes, a smaller one around my neck under my top, and the money for the day in my cargo pants pocket.

Monday morning we visited Edfu Temple dedicated to the falcon god Horus. As I learned about the many gods of this culture, I wondered how beliefs first began, who came up with these ideas and how did they get people to believe them? I know it began with the beginning of man and all cultures have participated in their own ways, but it still intrigues me.

By afternoon, we left Edfu to begin our journey to Aswan. The cruise down the Nile was incredible and extremely peaceful; it was my favorite part of the tour. I enjoyed sitting on the top deck watching Egypt go by, listening to the sounds, smelling the fragrances of cooking fires, burning weeds and sugar cane factories; and hearing the call to prayer from the Minarets. The call to prayer is done by a prayer leader whose voice is amplified by loud speaker from the top of the minaret, a very tall narrow tower beside or attached to the Mosque. I loved knowing that a lot of people in the area were praying at that moment, to the same God I pray to. I loved seeing the other riverboats and feluccas (small picturesque wooden sail boats) gliding down the river, and watching another world go by from my luxurious floating hotel.

Our two days in Aswan were so full, I can hardly remember which we did when, but it was all exciting and amazing. The Aswan Dam, also called the High Dam across the Nile, created Lake Nasser. This area of southern Egypt is home to the beautiful dark skinned Nubians. I could tell this culture was a bit different; women were much more visible. At the Nubian markets which specialized in jewelry and perfumes, women were working and most of our women indulged in the artistry of beautiful temporary Henna tattoos. Aswan is one of the driest inhabited places in the world; the last rain there was seven years ago and many local people don't even have roofs on part of their homes.

On Tuesday morning, we went sightseeing on the High Dam and visited the Temple of Isis, the Goddess of motherhood, magic and fertility. Ancient Egyptians believed that the Nile River flooded every year because of her tears of sorrow for her dead brother and husband, Osiris, but later because of her magical abilities, she was able to pick up the pieces of Osiris, put them back together and bring him back to life. We also visited the Unfinished Obelisk, carved directly out of bedrock at its quarry at Aswan. Although unfinished, it is the largest known ancient Obelisk and if finished, would have been one third larger. When cracks appeared in the granite, the project was abandoned, leaving unusual marks from tools and other insights into ancient Egyptian stone-working techniques. The highlight of our afternoon was a relaxing felucca boat trip on the Nile; I had so enjoyed watching these romantic wooden boats sailing the river, it was especially exciting to be sailing on one.

Wednesday morning we flew in a small passenger plane to the Great Temples of Abu Simbel. Other tourists made the 150 mile journey across the desert by bus from Aswan; a long line of busses fully surrounded by desert dust were just arriving as we were leaving. I was glad I had chosen the tour company that arrived by air before the crowd arrived by land. Probably because tourists had been shot there a few years ago, armed guards met the busses as they arrived, but were not obvious when we arrived by plane.

I was amazed at the size of these two massive temples of rock and the imposing statues at their entrances, but the most amazing thing was that this huge structure had been moved from its original location in the 1960's. Carved from a hillside by Pharaoh Ramesses II in the 13th century BC as a monument to himself and his Queen Nefertari, Abu Simbel was relocated, piece by piece, to prevent being submerged by Aswan Dam's creation of Lake Nasser, which also displaced a large population of Nubians.

As we cruised Wednesday night from Aswan to Kom-Ombo I slept well with the gentle rocking motion of the boat, until a call to prayer awoke me early and I looked out at the river. We were going by a felucca drifting downstream causing a perfect reflection in the water. I snapped a picture from the window of my room. Wide awake and too excited to return to bed, I climbed up on deck and enjoyed the fascinating rural landscape and the morning sounds and fragrances. One man of our group was up there already, and others began joining us an hour later.

Arriving at the agricultural town of Kom-Ombo by Thursday morning, we toured the two ancient Temples built in 2BC; the larger dedicated to Apollo; the smaller, to the sacred Isis. These imposing Ptolemaic period structures have remarkably retained their bright colors, which I guessed might be partially due to the extremely dry climate. A later addition was built by Tuthmosis III to honor the crocodile-headed god Sobek. Although our guide said crocodiles are no longer on this part of the Nile, crocodiles were sacred to the people of Ombos and many are mummified in the catacombs.

Our afternoon cruise to Luxor was an enchanting way to pass the time; our Gallebaya party that evening was a fun ending to a wonderful day, with dancing, wine, and lots of laughter.

Friday morning we went across the Nile River from Luxor to tour the monuments, temples, and tombs in the Valley of the Kings and the Valley of the Queens on the West Bank. On the nearby lower slopes, we passed numerous small Alabaster Factories, colorfully painted with murals and signs to entice tourists to stop in and buy souvenirs of this soft rock, hand-carved to produce any shape the mind can fathom. While we visited a factory, I walked around outside, catching glimpses of village life.

I absolutely loved walking around the Valley of the Kings or riding in their little open air shuttles. The tombs were underground and far from each other in the wide open spaces of a hilly desert landscape void of vegetation and creatures. I got the idea nothing grows there and because of the dry climate, nothing deteriorates there. Colorful pictures on the walls of the tombs have remained intact because they are underground with very little light and flashes from cameras were not permitted. Each tomb was cool, dark, and interesting, with the highlight being the Tomb of King Tut (Tutankhamun).

The Valley of the Queens is located a few miles from the Kings and is the resting place of Kings' families and a few Queens. I was especially intrigued by the imposing Temple of Queen Hatshepsut, but best of all I was captivated by being outside in the 104 degrees Fahrenheit desert air of Egypt. Although we were standing and walking in the sun with no breeze or clouds in the sky, I carried my water bottle, wore a hat, and felt quite comfortable. The dry air reminded me of Colorado and I loved it. I may also have been thawing out from the cold humid Berlin winter.

Friday evening we strolled through a bazaar in Luxor by ourselves. Instructing us to meet him at an outdoor café on the other end of the bazaar, our guide said we could safely split up; it was one very long narrow main street with open booths on both sides. Again, we were told to stay outside and never go in the back. Although I started out with the group, I ended up going at my own pace, taking in the exotic other-worldly feel; the sights, sounds, fragrances, smiling faces, friendly vendors, and the energy of happy people. Most of all, I was intrigued by the ground spices filling open bins, always shaped like an inverted cone. As soon as a purchase was dipped out, the vendor would re-shape the mound of spice, making it look full and untouched. At the cafe some of our group was smoking Hookah water pipes, usually with dried fruit and no tobacco. Although I didn't try it, those who did liked the apple taste and enjoyed the experience.

Saturday morning we paired up and rode horse drawn carriages all over Luxor through tiny little streets and in the busy marketplace. Little kids followed begging for money and trying to touch us; laughing and enjoying their quest. I was struck by the contrasting street scenes of modern high rise buildings, narrow alleys with clothes drying on lines strung high above, huge air conditioned busses, modern cars, horse-drawn carts, and men riding donkeys, bicycles, or walking barefoot dressed in traditional white Gallebayas and turbans.

We flew out of Luxor on Saturday evening for London. After riding the shuttle from Gatwick to Heathrow and spending the night at the airport, I arrived in Berlin Sunday morning at 11 am.

In retrospect, as I contemplate Egypt, one favorite memory is the morning I awoke at 4am; it was warm and I went up on the deck. The top deck wasn't lighted at night and I was able to be there alone and watch the bright stars—like in the Colorado Mountains. You know me; I find the nature part of the journey—and my solitude—even if it's when everyone else is asleep.

I also enjoyed seeing how the people lived, the bustling marketplaces with all the bargaining we had to do, and trying to stay away from the flirtatious men. Although I usually felt safe, I sometimes wished I had a fly swatter to keep the men off—they seemed like flies buzzing around! One day while walking around a market, I smelled a delightful fragrance which I assumed was incense. When I asked about it the men said it was weeds they burn to give off that pleasing aroma. They burnt some for me and had me walk around the small fire three times to make me more beautiful. The other women followed, we had fun, but guess what, it didn't work for me. I bought some of the weeds, but they lost their fragrance before I packed for the flight.

In the Ancient Egyptian temples, we saw evidence of Early Christians—crosses and a very old statue of Christ—the Christians took over some of the temples for awhile. Now they have some Christian Churches, called Coptic. The one we visited was in a very bad section of a small town and in very run down condition. The little barefoot boy who took us there had us winding all around the cobblestone and dirt streets for about a mile to get there. We tipped him well which, he reminded us at nearly ever corner, was required. Most all churches here are Muslim, but it's good Christians can still have their own churches if they want.

I asked our Egyptian tour guide, who spoke perfect English and was very well educated, about the culture and religious beliefs. My goal was to gain understanding, learn the truth as he sees it, and be more informed. I am most concerned about the treatment of women in Muslim cultures. He said Muslims worship the same God that Christians and Jews worship, so we have a strong link—I do agree with the link, but I cannot imagine God telling them to mistreat their women. I especially asked about the sexual mutilation of the women, as detailed by a Muslim woman in the book, *Desert Flower,* which I had read in Norway. He said that is not done much anymore; I hope he is right. I do like their strong family connections and that the men seem to honor their own mothers very much. Knowing Egypt and the United States were not currently on good terms, I asked his feeling about that. Just as Mustafa had told me in Turkey, he said his people don't like my government but they do like our people.

When we visited a large Mosque, we found it interesting that the men sat on the floor right in front of the leader, while women were much farther back, behind the men, in their own section. We asked our guide why they were so far from the leader; he told us it was to keep the men's minds on the message, instead of the women. After a week of hearing about Egyptian fertility, and witnessing the flirtatious men, I think I understand this custom.

Since our Spring Break was a lengthy two and a half weeks, I spent the second week in Tunisia, but that's another story for another day.

---

*That Gallebaya is still my favorite summer robe in 2010 and shows no wear yet.

From: Carol
To: LittleAli
Subject: **Relaxing in Tunisia**
Date: Sunday, May 6, 2001

With one day here to repack after returning from Egypt, I went to Tunisia by myself for a week. That was a German trip, on a German charter Plane, in a 4-star hotel with Germans, French, Italians, some British and no other Americans. This was definitely a resort area with a long line of hotels on the beach, as far as I could walk. After the whirlwind Egyptian trip and the fast pace of my daily life in Berlin, a luxurious week of walks on the beach and reading in the sun was just what I needed. I also had memories of the cruise to Tunisia my first year here and didn't feel it was a good place for a white foreign woman to explore alone.

On Tuesday, April 24, I took a taxi to Berlin's Schonefeld Airport for a departure at 3:30 am. Having never been to that airport (Berlin Tegel is the large one I have always used before), I was surprised it was so small and in such a dark section of town; the taxi driver seemed lost for awhile, but after studying his map, he got me there on time. Arriving in Monastir at 7 am, I rode the tour bus to the town of Port El Kantaou where I stayed at hotel Abou Newas Diar El Andalous on the Mediterranean Sea.

Walking barefoot along the beach and playing in the surf became my favorite pastime, especially because the sand was totally clean with no shells or other debris. I'm beginning to wonder if the Mediterranean has any shells, but I keep forgetting to ask. When not walking on the beach, I sat in the sun, swam in the warm indoor pool, read my book, and enjoyed the luxury of the 4-star hotel with many restaurants and shops. Breakfast buffet and dinner were included in the price. I usually had lunch at an outside café overlooking the Mediterranean Sea or at an outside pool. Sometimes lunch was only an ice cream sundae; such indulgence!

The boldly unique artwork decorating the hotel walls intrigued me, so when the artist had a show one evening, I bought one of his pieces in vivid primary colors painted on wood with designs from script of their Arabic language. He said my painting meant 'Peace'. I hope that's true. Another evening they had a showing and sale of works in leather with intricate textured designs. I loved the foot stools and bought one when I learned they were stuffed with pillows. It will make a good place to store extra pillows and rest my weary feet! Since the stool is just a leather shell, it fit easily into my luggage, along with the artwork.

The hotel staff was friendly and respectful; one waiter asked me out but when I declined, he graciously accepted that. I met one British woman about my age who joined me for dinner at the hotel every evening. Dinner was a special event and we all dressed up—I even wore pretty sun dresses and, although casual attire is usually my preference, actually enjoyed the elegance of the evening. It was fun having a friend to share the day's experiences. She was very gracious; we exchanged addresses, and I look forward to hearing from her again.

My return trip was Tuesday, May 1; a charter flight on Germania airline. Berlin is beautiful now and when we landed this time, I heard no groans but we all enthusiastically participated in the traditional cheering and clapping for the pilot and staff. The weather is warm and sunny with so much in bloom; we can eat outside at the cafes again. I love Berlin in the springtime!

So I'm back to work now and enjoyed all three days so far. Yesterday Lisa and I went to a Blossom Festival at Werner, two hours by boat from Wannsee. We enjoyed it so much last year; we just had to go back. The boat ride is so relaxing; it might be my favorite part. The festival was great and the local fruit wines in individual sized plastic bottles made it even better. This year I bought three dresses and a few other little things to remember this special town of blossoming fruit trees along the river Havel. Oh, did I tell you my beautiful Turkish outfit fell apart the second time I wore it? The fabric was delicate and the seams were a mere quarter of an inch and just couldn't take the stress of my moving body!

From: Carol
To: LittleAli
Subject: **Wrapping Things Up**
Date: Friday, May 18, 2001

The Kastania trees are in full bloom and I'm walking around in a daze, like I'm in love; but it's the place, the trees, the flowers, and the whole springtime atmosphere I'm in love with.

One of our German teachers, Katarina, invited some of us to her house for a barbeque. She lives in a very old house which has been in the family before and after the war. During the war it was taken over by the Gestapo and the family moved into what became West Berlin. The house is located just over the border in old East Berlin. Luckily the house survived the war and her family got it back. She and her daughter live on the first floor and her grandmother lives on the second floor. I was overwhelmed with the history and memories this magnificent old house hold. We had a wonderful time picnicking outside on this beautiful lawn in the warm Berlin evening and I felt so honored to have been invited to this comfortable gathering of friends.

As time for my return home gets closer, I have been asked and have considered staying another year. My vice principal keeps "begging" me to stay, and even came into my room one day with a rose, got down on one knee, and asked me to stay another year. He's funny and I think the request was sincere, but I had only planned to honor my 2-year contract. Being so far from family and friends takes its toll and being in surroundings where I understand conversations and can be understood, is appealing to me right now. There is one other consideration: the first two years teaching in Germany, Americans do not have to pay taxes in either country on what they earn here, so I have only been paying taxes on my retirement income in the United States. The third and subsequent years, we would pay German taxes, which makes sense and seems fair, but does deplete our income substantially; it would be just a little more than I made teaching in Colorado.

Not being able to understand conversations going on around me has had its advantages. I've been especially glad to not know what people are arguing about or saying with anger and loud voices. Somehow this lack of knowledge makes me feel sheltered from the cold cruel world and keeps me in a happy, detached world of childlike innocence.

I'm glad you got to be with your kids and grandkids on Mother's Day. I miss my girls but we did talk on the phone. My mother loved the tablecloth I bought her in Turkey. It fit her huge table perfectly! My health is much better now, I'm glad I didn't get that back operation. I walked five miles twice this week, but I don't know how I'll do at high altitude in the steep Colorado Rockies. That cross country ski hut trip you took into the mountains in March, pulling your backpack on a sled; sounds so beautiful and exciting; I will admit I'm jealous.

My last day of work is July 6. I have a small apartment lined up in Colorado Springs; I look it as a temporary place to live while I decide what's next. If I continue to be retired from Colorado, I can probably teach in any other state. I'm considering moving back to West Virginia to be near my parents, sisters, etc. and teach there. But I will take the rest of this year off at least. I asked a friend to move my stuff from storage into the new apartment so it will be somewhat ready when I get there. He will bring the key to you so I'll have a key if the office is closed. Thank you so much for saying I can stay with you for awhile, I certainly may want to do that the first night, as my flight gets in quite late. I'll rent a car and probably come to your house; I'm so excited to see you.

The shippers came May 6th for an estimate. It looks like I'll be shipping my stuff July 9th, and leaving here July 11th. The school has agreed to pay for the airfare and the shipping. The shippers will even pack for me, can you imagine? What a luxury! I packed myself when I came here, I didn't realize they would have paid then too. After that, I'll need to buy a car very soon; there's no reason to keep paying for a rental car. This time I'll be able to pay cash for a small car; I never thought I'd ever in my lifetime be able to buy a new car with cash!

On Memorial Day weekend I'll take a four day trip to Greece, on the island of Crete. Another adventure to look forward to!

From: Carol
To: LittleAli
Subject: **Dancing in Greece**
Date: Wed, May 30, 2001

For Memorial Day Weekend, from 5 am Friday morning, May 25th through Monday afternoon, May 28th, I was in Greece on the island of Crete. Arriving at Heraklion, the largest city and capital of Crete at 1 pm, I stayed in the town of Chersonisos, about a 20 minute taxi ride from Heraklion in a 4-star hotel on a beach.

This short four day stay in Crete was an exciting experience. One day I took a bus tour all over the island, through the mountains and to all four shores. I was thrilled with the beautiful scenery of rolling Olive tree covered hills and magnificent ocean beaches along rocky shores. We stopped at a pottery factory in Thrapsano and saw ancient clay artifacts of Minoan origin along with modern pottery being made by the best potters on the island. We were told pottery had been made in that area for the last eight centuries, a fact too overwhelming for me to imagine. I purchased a few beautiful small pieces of ancient looking vases. We were also given time to stroll through the picturesque Greek village of Ano Viannos with traditional stone homes of various colors on cobblestone streets, all adorned with tropical plants, trees, and flowers; an artist's paradise. Every building and street looked like a painting come to life.

My favorite excursion was an evening bus tour for a Cretan night out, with dancing in traditional costumes in the very old quaint small mountain village of Karouzanos on the side of a steep mountain with winding roads almost too narrow for our bus. Before the show and dinner, we had time to walk around this fascinating old world rural village with streets so steep I could hardly catch my breath. Artisans were selling their crafts in shops and on the streets. Each house was different and I was spellbound as I watched the villagers and wondered what daily life would be like on this vertical hillside. It was definitely a step back in time; years and years of time.

Before the show, a few hundred of us were served dinner of traditional local dishes in a huge building with a large stage for the performers. The first, last, and most often served was the *free* wine, with which we were taught to say *Opa* and clink our glasses before drinking each glass of wine. At my large table of 11 people, I was, as usual, the only solo tourist and the only American in the group. Although of different nationalities, we were somehow able to communicate and enjoy being together. We were entertained by musicians and dancers in traditional costumes. The dancers were all men and put on a fascinating and highly energetic performance for us—then they came down in the audience and each chose one person per table to join them in a traditional Greek dance all facing the same way, arms horizontally interlocked, step right-left-right, Kick, step left, Kick, around the room. Embarrassingly, I was the one chosen from my table. Although I didn't know how to do that dance, I quickly caught on and kept dancing as the professional dancers brought others into the group until everyone who was willing, was dancing in one very long line snaking through the tables and around the room. Finally, out of breath and still laughing, I was the last one to sit back down at our table. Before the meal, a photographer had taken our pictures, which we were able to see and purchase at the end of the evening; a keepsake to remember this special night in the mountains of Crete.

The narrow curvy road we came up must have been even more of a challenge for our bus driver as he drove down the steep grade late at night having no choice but to listen to us loudly singing all the songs we knew, with no opportunity to turn down the volume. . In a bus filled with Germans, Dutch, British, Scottish, and a few Americans—we sang—all the way down the mountain. It was a challenge finding songs everyone knew in the same language—and the only song we all knew and sang twice was John Denver's *Country Roads*. I had noticed Germans loved John Denver's songs and heard him often on the German radio stations in Berlin, so I wasn't too surprised at his universal popularity. Since I'm originally from West Virginia, *Country Roads* takes a special place in my heart. Although I usually tear up and can't sing it for the lump in my throat, I wasn't so emotional this time and enjoyed singing with the others.

Although my hotel was listed as a 4-star hotel, it was not as luxurious as any of the other 4-star hotels I've stayed in (including Nepal), but it was fine. I don't need luxury, and it was certainly better than the motels and cabins I stay in while traveling at home. And although my hotel was advertised as being on the beach, it wasn't. The beach was across the highway and was very rocky. I did wear sturdy shoes to walk along the beach although the rocks were dangerous; an easy place to slip and fall into the ocean below. The rocks and waves splashing on them created a beautiful rocky shore which I enjoyed with caution.

One afternoon I walked down to the village, looked through the shops, and bought a pretty blue cotton sundress with big flowers, which I wore to dinner at the hotel that night.

Although this trip was short, I enjoyed being there, seeing the country, taking the tours, and dancing and singing. Crete is a beautiful place; there are long difficult hiking trails I would have loved to try but didn't have the time. I would have loved to spend more time there, meet more of the local people, and learn more about their culture. I love their food, which is much like the Turkish food I enjoy so much.

Your hike from Aspen to Crested Butte with the *Wildflowers* sounds so magical! Which pass did you go over? That area has some of the most beautiful mountain scenery and spectacular wildflower displays in Colorado. And that helicopter ride back is such a 'civilized' idea.

From: Carol
To: LittleAli
Subject: **No Go!**
Date: Saturday, June 2, 2001

I planned to go to the German Alps this weekend on a night train, but stayed here instead! It's been raining ever since I got back from Crete, I caught a cold so I'm staying here and taking care of myself—basically looking forward to being lazy, drinking lots of juice, and feeling great by Tuesday when I return to work. The cold started after I got back from Crete, probably because there was no fresh air in the room at night, then coming back here to rain and 50 to 60 degree temperatures and a busy work week—more than my immune system could conquer, I guess.

I thought I'd be fine until yesterday at work when I was attack by a humongous headache, a fever, aches all over, and a cough in my chest. I decided it would not be fair to the other people in my sleeping car if I were blowing my nose and coughing all night—not to mention how miserable I would be doing all that on a train. So I called and cancelled the hotel reservations. No problem, I hadn't paid anything. And the train ticket can be turned in anytime. I think I only lose the reservation part of the payment, so I'm actually saving money. The forecast there was for cold rain Friday through Sunday; that was not enticing.

The liquids, rest, Echinacea, zinc, vitamin C and chicken soup all did their magic and now I'm ready for another work week and any other exciting events.

And I made a big mistake! There is a darling little gift shop near here in Zehlendorf which I love to go into. My mother collects owls. They have a beautiful collection of ceramic owls there. So I just bought mother the cutest owl in the store and sent it for Mothers' Day! Well, when we were talking on the phone and she had received the owl, she thanked me for it; then said, "You got me the same one last year, now I have two." She was so sweet about it, I just said, "Yes, they are a matched pair." And we went on with our conversation while I was falling apart inside! Can you imagine what an idiot I am??? Out of all the owls in the store, I picked the same one twice and didn't even remember! How many other foolish things have I been doing?

From: Carol
To: LittleAli
Subject: **Party Time!**
Date: Monday, June 25, 2001

The German Government has been taking Social Security from our paychecks, and most of us want to get that chunk of change back as soon as possible. Cindy and John, who have taught here before, went back to their Steamboat Springs, Colorado, home for awhile, are teaching here again. Knowing what we had to look forward to, they organized an Official German Form-Filling-Out Party to get us together, explain all the hoops we have to jump through to get our money, what letters and hassles we can expect, and how long we will probably wait to receive the official bank transfer. We must keep our German bank accounts open until our Social Security checks are deposited. That means we'll have small deductions for various fees taken out during this time, but in the end, we can close the account and have the money transferred to our new accounts, wherever we may be. Since the process will take about a year, with numerous communications throughout, we will also be able to contact the school secretaries for help through email and attachments of the official letters we can't understand; or when we just panic!

Our hosts will be in Zambia for their next teaching experience. Some friends will stay another year and others will be teaching in Mexico, Turkey, England, Sweden, France, and even in the United States. I am so thankful they took the time to explain this extremely complicated process in a foreign language of intimidatingly long German words to us—in the fun atmosphere of a party!

I love their apartment; it is so much more elegant than the plain ones the school chose for us. Since they had been here before, and had visited apartments of German friends, they were able to find a beautiful large apartment with character and convenience, huge windows, high ceilings; all the comforts of home in a beautiful old neighborhood. I have also visited apartments of German friends and have been amazed at the size, charm, character, architectural effects and how beautifully they have been decorated with huge indoor plants, prolific colorful flower garden balconies, and even indoor bedroom lofts. I will admit all of these are up several flights with no lifts or elevators, and I'm sure that's why Germans are in such good physical shape, not to mention all the walking and biking that is a necessary part of the daily life here. Although most Berliners don't own houses, their apartments are beautiful and offer an efficient and comfortable method of living for a large number of people in a city with little empty space.

Thank goodness the person moving into my apartment wants to purchase all my furniture, just like I bought the furniture that was here. Some of what I bought fell apart, and I have bought and put together more IKEA furniture, but the price comes to about the same $2000 I paid. It's such a help having all that in place for the new person, and such a relief for me to not have to try to sell it elsewhere and to not have to dispose of it somehow, somewhere!

Lisa is staying on another year but Laura is going to teach in Mexico and will be shipping her things (by boat) a month early. I'll be loaning her some stuff during that time. Luckily I don't have as much and can send it by air, which is soooo much faster! Most people have more and will ship the slow way, by ship.

Saturday I went to an elegant luncheon given by Cheryl, an American High School Teacher who has lived here many years and has made Germany her permanent home. There was a nice mix of German and American teachers. This time I got to be with more of the high school teachers than usual and really enjoyed visiting with them. The food was delicious, Cheryl's apartment was beautiful, the conversations were intriguing, and it was a fun afternoon. I felt honored to have been invited to this special event.

Two German Elementary teachers, Ina (pronounced E' na) and Kirsten (pronounced Keer' stin), gave an elegant Good Bye Party in Ina's beautiful apartment on 5th floor. I just can't get over how gracious, sweet, and interesting everyone is; in a fun and relaxing atmosphere. The balcony was so large and filled with flowers; we spent most of the evening in this outside garden high above the city.

I will miss so much about these two years here. Right now I'm thinking how I will miss going to Jenny's. Her physical therapy sessions have been so helpful I didn't need the back surgery. If I could take her with me, I might never need that surgery.* I will also miss the delightful Greek Restaurant near Jenny's office where I stop for dinner after her sessions. I love the music, ambience, food, and the wine. After Jenny's healing treatment and that meal, I feel relaxed and rejuvenated for the train/bus rides home and for the rest of the evening

---

*I had the back surgery in 2005 from an excellent West Virginia Neurosurgeon. It got rid of all the sciatic nerve pain, straightened my back, and allowed my leg muscles to work much better.

From: Carol
To: LittleAli
Subject: **Preparing to Leave**
Date: Friday, July 6, 2001

This was the last day of school, my last day to teach here; a gigantic milestone! The students, teachers, and administration were all so sweet and complimentary. I did shed a few tears, it was inevitable.

Lisa presented me with a scrapbook of memories from our adventures here. I could not believe how much time she took to include so many special places, events, and people. Then, she took it around to all the adults and asked them to sign it. They all wrote messages that left me speechless, so kind and complimentary and gracious; I could never have imagined such a treasure just for me!

A class of 4th graders wrote letters to me in German. Earlier, their teacher, Karin, had come with them to the computer room as scheduled, and said she had a writing assignment for them. As I helped them with their computer questions, I didn't notice anything about the content because it was in German; they printed the letters and Karin put them in a notebook and presented them to me in a later class session. She said I would need to get them translated before I left, which of course I did immediately. What sweet and complimentary messages they wrote; such a thoughtful gift, but most precious was the excitement of the children. They could hardly contain themselves when she presented it to me; it was such an exciting moment.

So many, probably all, the teachers, administrators, and secretaries stopped in to thank me for all I'd done for them and their students and had such personal stories of appreciation to share. Many of the students also stopped after classes to thank me and wish me good luck. I have never experienced such gratitude in all my years of teaching; I'm not sure it is deserved, but it is very appreciated.

I look forward to seeing you and my daughters, friends, and family soon. Erin will be working in the Creede Repertory Theater near Wolf Creek Pass in Colorado this summer, so I'll be going to see her as soon as possible and do more exploring in the mountains. Hopefully you and I will be able to hike some beautiful trails in August. Later, I'll be visiting Krysta in Baton Rouge, then my sister and her family in Atlanta around September 11*, and spend the rest of the fall in West Virginia with my parents, sisters, their families, aunts, cousins and friends; and traveling around that state. I haven't seen those brilliant fall colors for about 20 years and am really looking forward to it. While in West Virginia, I'll be looking for a place to live and plan to move there around the first of the new year. I'll probably be substitute teaching for the remainder of the school year there.

When I was 55 and on my first overseas trip, my roommate in Switzerland predicted I was catching the *Travel Bug* and this would be the beginning of many travel adventures for me. I disagreed, saying this was my once-in-a-lifetime outside the country travel. I would never be able to afford to travel again. I am so glad she was right and I was wrong!

I can't believe I've lived without a car, microwave, clothes dryer, window screens, or an air conditioner. I look forward to soon having all those and a washing machine that doesn't empty into the kitchen sink. It will be comforting to know that I can speak and be understood, to hear words I understand, and to read a sign and know its meaning. This experience has been wonderful and scary and challenging and amazing and difficult and refreshing and educational and thrilling and life-changing and eye-opening and filled with memories and friendships I will forever cherish.

Excited to see you July 12th! I'm coming home!

---

*I drove to Atlanta that tragic day, listening on the car radio from just after the first plane attack, in shock, and trying to see through my tears. At all my stops, I saw the horrific television scenes of the tumbling Twin Towers and people running in fear and panic. Driving into Atlanta around 3 pm, it was strangely empty; schools and businesses had been shut down. At a time when I craved being with family, all my family, it was good to be with my sister, but our minds seemed numb and everything felt surreal during that visit. Several days later, I was very relieved to see my parents in West Virginia, and know that my family was all safe, although we all felt the fear of not even knowing our enemies and the sadness of the tragedy that had hit so many of our countrymen.

CPSIA information can be obtained
at www.ICGtesting.com
Printed in the USA
BVOW06s2044100117
473132BV00016B/236/P

9 781453 899939